D0975063

Maryland's Historic Restaurants and Their Recipes

OTHER BOOKS IN THE HISTORIC RESTAURANTS SERIES™

Arizona's Historic Restaurants and Their Recipes
by Karen Mulford

Florida's Historic Restaurants and Their Recipes
by Dawn O'Brien and Becky Roper Matkov

Georgia's Historic Restaurants and Their Recipes
by Dawn O'Brien and Jean Spaugh

North Carolina's Historic Restaurants and Their Recipes
by Dawn O'Brien

Pennsylvania's Historic Restaurants and Their Recipes
by Dawn O'Brien and Claire Walter

South Carolina's Historic Restaurants and Their Recipes
by Dawn O'Brien and Karen Mulford

Virginia's Historic Restaurants and Their Recipes
by Dawn O'Brien

Maryland's Historic Restaurants and Their Recipes

by Dawn O'Brien
and Rebecca Schenck

Drawings by

Bob Anderson

and Patsy Faires

John F. Blair, Publisher
Winston-Salem, North Carolina

Copyright © 1995 by Dawn O'Brien and Rebecca Schenck
Printed in the United States of America
All Rights Reserved
Revised Edition
Original edition © 1985

DESIGN BY DEBRA LONG HAMPTON
MAP AND COMPOSITION BY LIZA LANGRALL
FRONT COVER PHOTOGRAPH BY GORDON SCHENCK
BACK COVER PHOTOGRAPH © 1990 BY LISA MASSON
PRINTED AND BOUND BY R. R. DONNELLEY & SONS

Library of Congress Cataloging-in-Publication Data

O'Brien, Dawn.
   Maryland's historic restaurants and their recipes / by Dawn O'Brien and
Rebecca Schenck.
      p.   cm.
   Includes index.
   ISBN 0-89587-137-8 (alk. paper)
   1. Cookery, American. 2. Cookery—Maryland. 3. Restaurants—
Maryland—Guidebooks 4. Historic buildings—Maryland.
   I. Schenck, Rebecca, 1931—   . II. Title.
TX715.0284   1995
641.59752—dc20   95-24800

*F*or my two sisters, Jessica Roubaud and Marian Daugherty, who keep asking, "When are you going to dedicate a book to me?" This is it, girls!

Dawn O'Brien

*F*or the families represented by these restaurants and for my own family — especially Gordon.

Rebecca Schenck

Foreword

"A good cook is a sorceress who dispenses happiness," said designer Elsa Schiaparelli. In the early days of my marriage, my cooking produced happiness—that is, if you equate giggles with happiness. In fact, my husband, John, still laughs about our first Thanksgiving. Having bought a "stuffed turkey" in the supermarket, I thought, "Oh, good, I won't have to make stuffing." Yes, indeed, old dummy actually cooked that bird with its own innards! Was it terrible? No, the turkey was quite moist and tasty. But that was seven cookbooks ago, before I realized that creativity in the kitchen is often what your imagination can salvage from disaster.

You see, I am basically a lazy writer who is hooked on history. I say lazy because I prefer to do research in epicurean restaurants rather than in stuffy libraries. Especially when half of the research consists of delighting my taste buds with the creativity of the world's finest chefs. Yes, I know: "It's a tough job but somebody has to do it." What makes this work intriguing is that each state—in fact, each restaurant—is so different. But after eating myself through North Carolina's, Virginia's, South Carolina's, Pennsylvania's, Georgia's, and Florida's historic restaurants, I realized that the limitations of time necessitated collaborators for the series. Hence, I began looking for other lazy—or, shall we say, sensually indulgent—writers who are also into the *joie de vivre*.

For this book, co-author Rebecca Schenck—along with her architectural photographer husband, Gordon—and I have enjoyed Maryland's contrasts in fine food. We found Maryland abundant in its culinary selections. Gordon, who uncomplainingly vows that he has tasted Maryland seafood prepared in every possible way, is convinced that this seafood is the tenderest that has ever crossed his palate, particularly the Romaine-Wrapped Fillet of Salmon at Oxford House Restaurant at The Inn at Walnut Bottom. My daughter Heather, on the other hand, votes for the dynamite desserts, especially Antrim 1844's Chocolate Pâté.

My daughter Daintry was surprised that a novice cook like herself could actually duplicate such masterpieces as The Penwick House's Mushroom Turnover. From the beginning, that was one of my goals: to put unusually delicious recipes in a form that could easily be followed at home. It is creativity, not fancy cooking-school technique, that makes an ordinary cook into an extraordinary cook. The recipes included here may seem simple, but the creative touches of the chefs guarantee delicious results.

In collecting these recipes, Rebecca and I have been tutored by chefs who have studied at the famous cooking schools of the world. But these chefs are quick to point out that education was only one important ingredient in their success. Talent lies in starting with the basics and creating one's own thing.

Rebecca and I have tried to follow that course in this book. Our "basics" begin with restaurants housed in buildings that are over fifty years old. At that age or older, a structure generally has a good story to tell. In visiting these restaurants, we "do our own thing." We try to find the most intriguing story that the establishment has to offer and then weave that story in with our impressions of the food, decor, and ambiance. After sampling the restaurant's most popular offerings, we select several recipes, which we take home to test. People often ask, "Why do you test every recipe if you've already eaten it at the restaurant?" The reason is simple: we must make sure that ingredients are correctly proportioned for home use and that the recipes are easy to follow.

We found that many of Maryland's historic restaurants have been in the same family for generations. We've met parents and children working together in restaurants inherited from past generations.

Rebecca confides that she expected the best part would be hearing and writing the stories, but now she feels that the best part comes from meeting the people who tell those stories. In these times of family polarity, we can't think of a nicer way to remember a state than to associate it with warm, family-accented stories. When we return home, we come not only with a new batch of recipes, but a new batch of people who have touched our lives in a special way.

Acknowledgments

$\mathcal{B}$ooks like this don't just happen. A lot of people get in on the act. Researching the research comes first—that is, contacting the many agencies and societies within a state to find out where to go and what to look for. We are thankful to those who pointed us in the right direction and to many others who paved the roads for us in a variety of ways.

To: Anne Mannix, publication/marketing coordinator, Office of Tourism Development, Maryland Department of Economic and Employment Development, who opened paths for us to follow.

To: The Maryland chambers of commerce, tourism councils, and public libraries, and in particular to Betty C. Callahan, Kay Morrow, Betty S. Stilt, Norma Grovermann, Jo Beynon, Cindy Kutchman, and Richard Parsons, who did extra paving.

To: Gil Stotler, assistant director of tourism and promotion, Baltimore Area Convention and Visitors Association.

To: Patricia Pipozar, executive secretary, Kent County Chamber of Commerce.

To: Wayne Hill, Hill's Holiday Travel, Cecil County.

To: Diane Molnar, director, Baltimore County Conference and Visitors Bureau.

To: Barbara Beverungen, senior tourism assistant, Carroll County.

To: Jeanne Vasold, executive director, Tourism Council of Frederick County.

To: Lisa Challenger, director, Worcester County Tourism.

To: Michele Brinsfield, marketing, Allegany County Visitors Bureau and Information Center.

To: Kathy Magruder, director, Queen Anne's County Visitor Service.

To: The staff at Enoch Pratt Free Library in Baltimore for their aid in research.

To: Doug Zima, who scouted out restaurants that we would not otherwise have found.

To: The chefs, who generously shared their time, talent, and secrets with us.

To: The restaurateurs, who often did as much digging as we did in tracing stories.

To: The artists Bob Anderson and Patsy Faires, who did such a splendid job with their pen-and-ink renderings.

To: The editors Ginny Hege, Sue Clark, and Steve Kirk, who edited with sensitivity, skill, and kindness.

To: Daintry O'Brien, who helped with the driving, photography, and testing of recipes.

To: Gordon Schenck for our beautiful cover shot, as well as for his help with testing and tasting.

To: All our guinea pigs (old and new to the series), who continue to flatter our efforts.

Contents

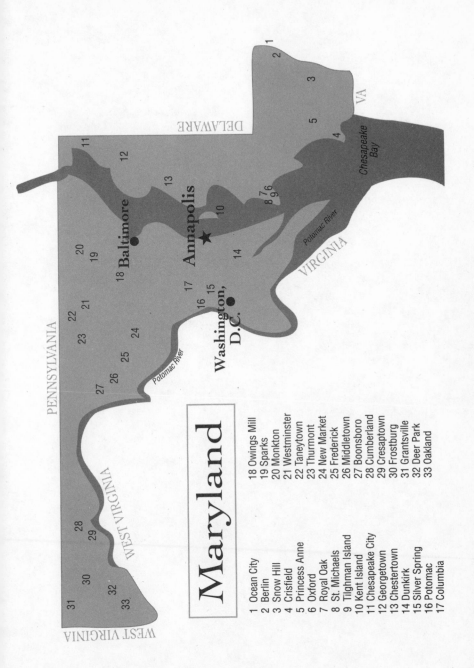

Maryland

1 Ocean City
2 Berlin
3 Snow Hill
4 Crisfield
5 Princess Anne
6 Oxford
7 Royal Oak
8 St. Michaels
9 Tilghman Island
10 Kent Island
11 Chesapeake City
12 Georgetown
13 Chestertown
14 Dunkirk
15 Silver Spring
16 Potomac
17 Columbia
18 Owings Mill
19 Sparks
20 Monkton
21 Westminster
22 Taneytown
23 Thurmont
24 New Market
25 Frederick
26 Middletown
27 Boonsboro
28 Cumberland
29 Cresaptown
30 Frostburg
31 Grantsville
32 Deer Park
33 Oakland

PENNSYLVANIA

WEST VIRGINIA

WEST VIRGINIA

DELAWARE

VA

VIRGINIA

VIRGINIA

Chesapeake Bay

Potomac River

Potomac River

Baltimore

Annapolis

Washington, D.C.

Maryland's Historic Restaurants and Their Recipes

Commander Hotel

Fourteenth Street, on the ocean
OCEAN CITY

" *Y*ou'll never make a go of it — it's too far out of town," John Lynch was told when he built the Commander Hotel in 1930. It was on the ocean at Fourteenth Street, and the boardwalk ended at Fifteenth. Now, a strip of high-rise hotels and resort condominiums extends another hundred blocks, and John Lynch, Jr., accepts reservations two to three years in advance.

Breakfast
8:00 A.M. until 10:00 P.M.
Daily
Mid-April until Mid-October

Dinner
6:00 P.M. until 8:00 P.M.
Daily
Mid-April until Mid-October

For reservations
(not necessary)
call (410) 289-6166

Ocean City used to be a part of Assateague Island, the "place across," as Indians called the beautiful reef between the Atlantic and the mainland of Maryland and Virginia. The island embodies the mystery of shipwrecks, pirates, and wild ponies. For centuries, its shoreline has been determined by wind and ocean. In 1933, a hurricane cut a channel at Ocean City and caused people to remember that "it is an ill wind turns none to good." Ocean City Inlet is considered a major factor in the growth of the seaside resort. During some months of the year, Ocean City is now the second-most-populated city in Maryland.

I ate in an L-shaped dining room whose bentwood chairs had slipcovered backs to match the draperies at the shuttered windows. The walls in the room are "pulled" stucco — no paint — with a whiter lime on the ceiling. I could see why the room was selected to be in a motion picture.

The relaxing decor, with its just-right touches of cheerful pink and green, will make you want to linger over coffee and another Coconut Muffin at breakfast, or Southern Spoonbread on Friday mornings that would satisfy even your aunt Mary, or a Rum Bun after dinner — all baked in the Commander's kitchen.

People return to the Commander Hotel year after year for family vacations and business conventions, knowing they can expect good food and comfort. The Knights of Columbus have come for thirty years. When I arrived — along with 250 "St. John's Oldtimers" — the Maryland Soft-Drink Bottlers had just left. There was a hubbub in the lobby, and I picked up a sheet at the desk announcing an Irish Wake Story Contest for the Oldtimers, to be judged by the oldest ones among them. I asked for an example of a story. The contest's originator didn't want to give away the best, but he offered this: "Did you know Frank?" "No, but he's got a lovely set of teeth."

Poor Frank, if he didn't get to sink them into the Peach Brandy Pound Cake. The family of John Lynch, Jr., has this melt-in-your-mouth cake at home every Christmas. The cake is also a regular offering on the menu for the Commander's Boardwalk Cabaret, which operates at the Commander Hotel five nights a week during July and August. I hope to make a reservation soon.

I have a day all planned. I'll lie on the beach until I've had enough sun. Then I'll browse in shops along the boardwalk, already knowing the way to Newmyer's in the Commander's basement, where I'll get a Waffle Cone or Peanut Brittle. After a nap, I'll enjoy the player piano in the Skipjack Lounge until the pianist comes to the baby grand. A glass of Mateus Rosé will prepare me for dinner.

COMMANDER HOTEL'S PEACH BRANDY POUND CAKE

1 cup butter	2 teaspoons rum
3 cups sugar	1 teaspoon orange extract
6 eggs	1/4 teaspoon almond extract
3 cups all-purpose flour	2/3 teaspoon lemon extract
1/4 teaspoon baking soda	1 teaspoon vanilla extract
pinch of salt	1/2 cup peach brandy
1 cup sour cream	

Cream butter and gradually add sugar, beating well. Add eggs 1 at a time, mixing well after each addition. Combine flour, soda, and salt; add to creamed mixture alternately with sour cream, beating well after each addition. Stir in remaining ingredients. Pour batter into a well-greased and floured 10-inch Bundt pan or tube pan. Bake at 325 degrees for 1 hour and 20 minutes or until cake tests done. Yields 1 cake.

COMMANDER HOTEL'S CAPTAIN JACK'S CARROT SALAD

6 cups canned, sliced carrots
1 green pepper, chopped
1 small onion, chopped
10-ounce can tomato soup
¾ cup sugar
1 teaspoon prepared mustard

1 teaspoon Worcestershire
　sauce
¾ cup cider vinegar
1 teaspoon salt
4 tablespoons salad oil
1 teaspoon black pepper

Mix all ingredients and chill overnight. Keeps well in refrigerator in a 3-quart covered casserole. Serves 12.

COMMANDER HOTEL'S SOUTHERN SPOONBREAD

1 pint milk
1 teaspoon salt
⅔ cup water-ground white
　cornmeal

1 tablespoon sugar
2 tablespoons margarine
3 eggs
2 teaspoons baking powder

In a large saucepan, heat milk, salt, cornmeal, sugar, and margarine, stirring to prevent lumps, until the mixture is the consistency of stiff mush. Remove from heat and stir until mixture cools. Break eggs 1 at a time into mixture and stir hard after each addition. Add baking powder. Pour batter into a greased 3-quart baking dish or any pan that fills with batter to a depth of about 4 inches. Bake at 375 degrees for 30 to 40 minutes. Serves 8 to 10.

Note: Finished product should be moist, *not* dry like cornbread. It is traditionally served with a spoon. Do not use a shallow pan, or spoonbread will be too dry.

Atlantic Hotel

2 North Main Street
BERLIN

erlin's Main Street might have been an Edward Hopper painting or one of Norman Rockwell's *Saturday Evening Post* covers. Brick buildings with interesting shapes and decorative features—turrets, stained glass, stamped metal cornices—house antique shops, a barbershop, a hardware store, and a soda fountain. And standing proud again on one prominent corner is the Atlantic Hotel, built in 1895.

Main Street used to be part of the path connecting the Assateague Indians with the neighboring Pocomoke tribe. In colonial times, the path became the Philadelphia Post Road, the main travel route up the Eastern Shore. The village of Berlin grew around a three-hundred-acre land grant dating from 1677; the land later became Burley Plantation. The name Berlin might have come from a contraction of Burleigh Inn, a tavern on the Philadelphia Post Road.

In the early 1900s, Berlin had more hotels than Ocean City did, and the Atlantic Hotel was popular with traveling salesmen—"drummers"—until hard times hit. In the 1980s, a group of interested citizens formed the Atlantic Hotel Partnership to restore the hotel, a project that earned a State Historic Trust Preservation Award.

From the time of the hotel's original opening, the dining room had a reputation for fine local delicacies such as diamondback terrapin. I thought of that when the executive chef gave me a recipe for Snapper Turtle Soup. I questioned the availability of snapper turtles, and someone recalled that a police chief used to bring them to the restaurant to be cooked. I was so pleased with the Seafood Bisque I had for dinner that I sent a request to the kitchen for that recipe, too.

The chef credited the Atlantic Hotel Partnership's first chef, Stephen Jacques, with establishing the hotel's signature dishes. I had read of Jacques' earlier days with the Joffrey Ballet, and I asked where he was now. "At the seminary," said our helpful waitress, who told us

Meals
Noon until 9:00 P.M.
Monday through Thursday
Noon until 10:00 P.M.
Friday and Saturday
11:00 A.M. until 2:00 P.M.
4:00 P.M. until 9:00 P.M.
Sunday
For reservations
(suggested for dinner)
call (410) 641-3589

that Stephen's wife designed the wine label for the hotel's hundredth anniversary. Gordon and I toasted them with a glass of Poppy Hill Chardonnay.

Without deciding which of our entrées was better, Salmon en Croûte or Blackened Redfish, we ended with the Atlantic Hotel's signature dessert, Bailey's Irish Cream Cheesecake.

We had only to climb the stairs to go to bed. Our corner room was furnished with a marble-topped dresser, an armoire, a love seat, vintage prints, and the tallest headboard I've ever propped myself against. Decorators scoured the Delmarva Peninsula for antiques true to the region.

After a solid night's sleep, we went to the Drummer's Cafe, where less formal meals are served and hotel guests help themselves to hot Croissants and Scrambled Eggs for breakfast. Those drummers from the early days would have liked this place.

ATLANTIC HOTEL'S SEAFOOD BISQUE

1 pound shrimp, peeled and deveined, shells saved
1 teaspoon oil
4 cups water
7 tablespoons unsalted butter
1 cup leeks, white part only, cleaned
1/2 pound mushrooms, sliced thin
1/3 cup parsley, chopped

1/4 cup flour
1/4 pound scallops
1/4 pound flaky white fish (flounder, cod, orange roughy)
1 cup heavy cream
3/4 cup plum tomatoes, puréed
1/3 cup dry sherry
salt and pepper to taste
fresh dill for garnish

Sauté shrimp shells in oiled pan until bright red; add water and simmer for 10 minutes. Strain to remove shells; save liquid. Melt butter with leeks, mushrooms, and parsley until vegetables are clear. Add flour, cooking lightly to make a roux. Pour in reserved liquid from shrimp shells, stirring constantly. Add seafood and cook at low temperature until seafood is done. Add heavy cream, tomato purée, and sherry. Adjust salt and pepper and garnish with dill. Serves 6.

ATLANTIC HOTEL'S BAILEY'S IRISH CREAM CHEESECAKE

Crust

2 cups crushed Oreo cookies   ⅛ cup chocolate chips
¼ cup melted butter

Mix cookies and butter and press into bottom and 1 inch up the sides of a springform pan. Bake at 325 degrees for 7 to 10 minutes. Sprinkle chocolate chips inside pan.

Filling

2¼ pounds cream cheese   6 eggs
1½ cups sugar   1 tablespoon vanilla
1 cup Bailey's Irish Cream   ¼ cup semisweet chocolate

Whip all ingredients except chocolate until smooth, being careful not to overmix. Pour batter into crust and bake at 250 degrees in water bath for 90 minutes until set. Put in a cool place and let sit for 3 hours before releasing springform. Melt chocolate and garnish top. Yields 1 cheesecake.

Snow Hill Inn

104 East Market Street
SNOW HILL

In the walking tour of a hundred historic houses in the town of Snow Hill, founded in 1642, something might stop you outside a cast-iron gate that still bears the name of Dr. John S. Aydelotte. It might be what a 1993 story in the *Baltimore Sun* called "The Ghost With Inn," about a bizarre event that happened to the family that lived in the house at the turn of the century. John Aydelotte was the town doctor, and his son William was a student at the Maryland

Lunch
11:00 A.M. until 2:00 P.M.
Monday through Saturday

Dinner
5:30 P.M. until 9:00 P.M.
Wednesday through Saturday

4:00 P.M. until 8:00 P.M.
Sunday

For reservations
(suggested)
call (410) 632-2102

School of Pharmacy when he was discovered dead under mysterious circumstances in 1904. Whether he committed suicide or not, William was a troubled soul. Perhaps his spirit wanders in his homeplace, now Snow Hill Inn. Folks here sometimes see lights flicker or hear noises which cause innkeeper-chef Jim Washington to say noncommittally, "Oh, that's just J. J."—the ghost's nickname. "Don't mind him."

Snow Hill, the county seat of Worcester County, was made a Royal port in 1694. Situated on the banks of the Pocomoke River, it calls itself "the Undiscovered Treasure of the Eastern Shore." When I asked about the population—which currently stands at 2,400—Jim Washington said his daughter became the 2,022nd person when she was born after the family moved to Snow Hill.

Talking about the restaurant, Jim said, "We care about each customer." Of course, that causes customers to return often. In fact, a woman sitting at a table outside told me she could make it through the workweek better if she ate lunch at least once at Snow Hill Inn. Another said she almost always orders the Crab Quiche.

Gordon and I stopped at Snow Hill Inn for lunch, parking in the lot behind the building and passing by a flower bed bordered by jagged bricks—like the flower beds in my backyard childhood—to enter the room that's most popular at midday. Gordon ordered Crab Quiche and I an Oyster Sandwich; we were glad to see those listed on the blackboard as specials. We enjoyed the dressings on our salads, too: Blue Cheese and the House Dressing, which was Catalina with onion and cucumber.

Kitchen workers were busily preparing box lunches for courthouse employees and others nearby who had ordered takeout specials; that day, it was Spinach Salad or Ham Steak with Broccoli and Potatoes. Jim said he puts a little sugar and nutmeg in the water when steaming broccoli. He sautés carrots with thyme, lemon juice, and white wine.

A muffin is packed in each takeout box, just as a basket of muffins is brought first thing to every table. Jim calls himself "the Ben and Jerry of Muffins," adding peaches, strawberries, bananas, and other fruits to the batter. He likes to bake breads and asked us if we remembered "five-and-ten" bread from the 1940s, which contained five seeds and ten herbs. Already feeling nostalgic, I became aware that I was hearing Jimmy Durante's voice singing "As Time Goes By" in the background.

Light fare is served in the Lounge, which has a separate entrance at the front of the house. I peeked in one of the inn's upstairs bedrooms and saw nothing amiss, just a wicker bed, chairs, and lamp, along with an iron daybed under the sloped ceiling. A tray with two small bottles of wine and glasses awaited the next occupants; I can't say whether J. J. was waiting, too.

SNOW HILL INN'S COCONUT CUSTARD PIE

6 eggs, beaten
1 cup heavy cream
1 cup sugar

1½ cups coconut flakes
2 tablespoons coconut
   flavoring
1 9-inch pie shell

Combine first 5 ingredients, stirring until well blended. Pour into unbaked pie shell and bake at 375 degrees for 35 minutes or until lightly browned. Yields 1 pie.

SNOW HILL INN'S CRAB QUICHE

1 sheet puff pastry
5 eggs, beaten
1 cup heavy cream
8 ounces sharp cheddar cheese, grated

6 ounces Swiss cheese, grated
½ teaspoon seafood seasoning
1 teaspoon cilantro, chopped
¾ pound crabmeat

Fit puff pastry into a large pie pan. Combine eggs, cream, and cheeses. Add seasonings and stir in crabmeat. Pour into pastry shell and bake at 375 degrees for 45 minutes or until a knife inserted in center comes out clean. Serves 8.

SNOW HILL INN'S APPLE RAISIN MUFFINS

4½ cups flour
1½ cups sugar
1 tablespoon baking powder
1½ teaspoons nutmeg
1½ teaspoons cinnamon

2¼ cups milk
2 eggs, beaten
4 tablespoons butter, melted
1 large apple, peeled, cored, and chopped coarse
¼ cup raisins

Mix first 5 ingredients, then stir in milk and eggs. Add butter, apple, and raisins. Combine well and pour into muffin tins. Bake at 375 degrees for 15 to 20 minutes. Yields 2 dozen muffins.

Captain's Galley

1021 West Main Street
CRISFIELD

big red crab painted on a water tower was our advance notice that Crisfield is called "the Crab Capital of the World." My husband, Gordon, and I drove into town on a Sunday morning to take a ferry to Smith Island. Next to the city dock, I noticed that the *New York Times* was mentioned on a sign above a building. Thinking I might buy a copy of that paper, I

Meals
8:00 A.M. until 9:00 P.M.
Sunday through Thursday
8:00 A.M. until 10:00 P.M.
Friday and Saturday
For reservations
(accepted)
call (410) 968-1636

walked up to the building. On closer inspection, however, I found that the building was a restaurant called Captain's Galley. The *New York Times* was listed because it had reviewed the restaurant—favorably, I might add.

Another sign that hangs over the building reads, "Best Crab Cakes in the World." Since we had time to spare before catching the *Island Belle*, which is also the mailboat, we went into Captain's Galley for a cup of coffee. From the restaurant at the foot of Main Street, we could look out on Tangier Sound and see the boat we were to board.

We learned that tracks of the Pennsylvania Railroad used to be in the middle of Main Street, built on oyster shells. In the 1930s, the restaurant building served as a wholesale fish house, and in the 1940s, it was a crab-picking plant. Later, it became a restaurant—specializing in seafood, naturally, since seafood has always been the main industry in Crisfield.

Gordon and I did ride to Smith Island. We enjoyed being on waters charted by Captain John Smith in 1608. We felt that we had been drawn back in time ourselves when we docked at Ewell and walked to another restaurant in a house whose "address" was "the second house beyond the church."

When we returned to Crisfield, we went back to Captain's Galley for Crabmeat Salad, the good taste of which I remembered for days, and a sampling of the appealing Salad Bar, made out of a crab float. Large, clear bowls were set in ice, with spiced apple rings scattered around them like life preservers. Green and red tomatoes, green and red peppers, green and red beans, radishes that looked like peppermints—these and other salad vegetables and greens were arranged alongside the dressings and loaves of bread.

Since our first visit, Captain's Galley has taken its Crab Cakes on the road with a concession trailer called "The Crab Cake Express." This kitchen on wheels, which travels to fairs and festivals held within a reasonable distance and to private parties and picnics, can quickly serve large groups of people. Captain's Galley also has a store next door to the restaurant, where customers can buy jars of the "Captain's Gourmet Mixin's" to take home and add to crabmeat when they want to fix crab cakes themselves.

Before we left Captain's Galley, we read the publicity in the lobby. I agree with what the *New York Times* said: "Anyone who won't eat a crab is one."

CAPTAIN'S GALLEY'S BROILED BACKFIN CRABMEAT

¾ pound backfin crabmeat
dash of Old Bay seasoning
¼ cup Sauterne

3 tablespoons butter
parsley flakes

Pick shells out of crabmeat. Place crabmeat in individual casserole dishes. Lightly sprinkle Old Bay seasoning over crabmeat and pour 2 tablespoons of Sauterne over each dish. Dot with butter, sprinkle with parsley flakes, and broil for 10 minutes. Serves 2.

CAPTAIN'S GALLEY'S SPICY ONE

3 8-ounce flounder or trout
fillets
¼ teaspoon salt
1½ teaspoons Old Bay
seasoning

1½ teaspoons paprika
4 tablespoons lemon juice
¼ teaspoon parsley flakes
3 tablespoons butter
lemon slices

Place fillets in a baking dish and sprinkle with salt, Old Bay seasoning, and paprika. Sprinkle with lemon juice and top with parsley. Dot with butter and broil for 12 to 15 minutes or until fish flakes easily. Garnish with lemon slices. Serves 3.

CAPTAIN'S GALLEY'S CRABMEAT SALAD

½ cup mayonnaise
¾ teaspoon Old Bay seasoning
¼ teaspoon Worcestershire
*   sauce*

dash of hot sauce
2 cups backfin crabmeat,
*   picked*
¾ cup diced celery

Whisk mayonnaise, Old Bay seasoning, Worcestershire sauce, and hot sauce into a smooth mixture. In a large bowl, gently combine crabmeat and celery. Spoon mayonnaise mixture over crabmeat and lightly blend. Serves 4 to 6.

Hotel Inn Restaurant and Lounge

Washington Hotel, 11782 Somerset Avenue
PRINCESS ANNE

$\mathcal{S}$ ome people don't believe in coincidence. Was it fate, then, that brought Gordon and me to meet Mary Murphey, owner of the Washington Hotel, shortly after we had bought an artist's print entitled *Mary Murphy*? Fate seemed compatible with the strong sense of history in the hotel, which has been in continuous operation since 1744.

The lobby has two staircases: one for women in hoop skirts, the other for men. Photographs are segregated, too: United States presidents on one wall, first ladies on another. We had a room at the top of the stairs where Basil Rathbone spent the night when he appeared in a play at the University of Maryland-Eastern Shore. Some rooms have been modernized, but Mary Murphey says guests prefer old furnishings. She is proud of the family antiques in her living quarters downstairs. From a 1789 ledger she showed us, I learned that two gallons of brandy were considered fair pay for one day's work.

In the Hotel Inn, managed by Mrs. Murphey's son, we were seated in the dining room that honors Judge Samuel Chase, a signer of the Declaration of Independence from the town of Princess Anne. I recognized "a large mahogany sideboard (very valuable)" as being the one listed in a 1900 inventory of furniture which Mary Murphey had shown us. It was made more valuable for me by holding baskets of gaillardia daisies flanked by old wine bottles.

A party of sixteen people at one end of the room was offering toasts. I learned that it was a fiftieth wedding anniversary party, a celebration all the more special because the couple had been married at the Washington Hotel.

Our waitress said that the party was being served one of the restaurant's most popular dishes, Seafood Imperial, which was not on the menu that night. We asked if we could have it, too, and were glad we did; it was spicy and full of shrimp.

Breakfast
6:00 A.M. until 11:00 A.M.
Monday through Saturday

Lunch
11:00 A.M. until 4:00 P.M.
Monday through Saturday

Dinner
4:00 P.M. until 9:00 P.M.
Monday through Saturday

For reservations
call (410) 651-2526

The Hotel Inn's cuisine is local Eastern Shore seafood. Dinners include a salad and two vegetables. We chose four different vegetables and decided that our favorite was the Stewed Tomatoes, with their cinnamon-nutmeg flavor.

As we ate, a young couple was seated near us. He wore a red rose boutonniere and she an orchid corsage. Although I tried not to intrude by staring, I admired their happy good looks and noticed what they ordered: Pecan Pie for him, Blueberry Pie à la Mode for her. Finally, I spoke, and my suspicions were confirmed—it was their wedding day. I found it a coincidence that Gordon and I, seated between the newlyweds and the fifty-year celebrants, had been married twenty-five years. To honor that coincidence, we had a dessert with a wedding flavor—Rice Custard.

On Sunday morning when we were leaving the hotel, I saw on the floor in front of the register a grain of rice and a flower from the bride's bouquet.

HOTEL INN RESTAURANT AND LOUNGE'S SEAFOOD IMPERIAL

1 egg
1 tablespoon dry mustard
1 tablespoon Old Bay seasoning
1 teaspoon Worcestershire sauce

3 tablespoons mayonnaise
2 jumbo shrimp, peeled and deveined
1 pound crabmeat

In a bowl, beat the egg and add mustard, Old Bay seasoning, Worcestershire sauce, and mayonnaise. Cut shrimp in small pieces and mix into crabmeat. Gently mix crabmeat with egg mixture. Pour into a baking dish. Dot with butter and bake in a 350-degree oven for 25 minutes. Serves 4.

HOTEL INN RESTAURANT AND LOUNGE'S
STEWED TOMATOES

2 16-ounce cans tomatoes
1 cup sugar
2 teaspoons nutmeg
2 teaspoons cinnamon

3 slices stale bread, cubed
1 tablespoon butter
cornstarch

Mash tomatoes in a saucepan. Add sugar, nutmeg, cinnamon, bread, and butter. Simmer mixture on stove until flavors are well blended. Add cornstarch to thicken as desired. Serves 4 to 6.

HOTEL INN RESTAURANT AND LOUNGE'S
RICE CUSTARD

4 eggs
½ cup sugar
1 quart milk
pinch of salt
1 teaspoon vanilla

¾ cup cooked rice
whipped cream
nutmeg
cinnamon

Beat eggs and sugar together. Add milk, salt, vanilla, and rice. Bake in a greased 9- by 13-inch pan for 1 hour at 350 degrees. Serve warm or cold, topped with whipped cream and sprinkled with nutmeg and cinnamon. Serves 10 to 12.

Note: This dish will keep in the refrigerator for up to a week.

Robert Morris Inn

Tred Avon River
OXFORD

$\mathcal{D}$ oesn't everyone look back with regret on some missed opportunity? A friend of mine once had the chance to buy the Robert Morris Inn but had to pass it up. Things might have been different if he could have borrowed the money on his honor, as Robert Morris, Jr., did to finance the Continental Army.

Robert Morris, Sr., the father of that Revolutionary War financier, died before the American Revolution, the victim of a freak accident. Wadding from a ship's guns being fired in his honor struck him and proved fatal. The house he lived in is now the Rob-

Breakfast
8:00 A.M. until 11:00 A.M.
Wednesday through Monday

Lunch
Noon until 3:00 P.M.
Wednesday through Monday

Dinner
6:00 P.M. until 9:00 P.M.
Wednesday through Monday

Noon until 9:00 P.M.
Sunday

Reservations not accepted
(410) 226-5111

ert Morris Inn. It was built by ships' carpenters before 1710 and bought by an English trading company in 1730 as a residence for Morris, who represented the company's interests in Oxford.

The Robert Morris Inn is doing well with the motto "Quality is Our Tradition." Owners Wendy and Ken Gibson invite their guests to experience that tradition in a tranquil atmosphere: wonderful food, a reading room, walks by the Tred Avon River, and a ride on America's oldest ferry, the Oxford-Bellevue, established in 1683.

Gordon and I ate in the tavern, which has a slate floor, brick booths, and the Morris coat of arms over the fireplace. With a glass of good iced tea (never to be taken for granted) in hand, we looked over the menu. Since twenty of the twenty-seven entrées were seafood, we ordered a Seafood Sampler.

The Crab, attractively served on a ruffle of kale, was what we went for first. It was so good that we both saved some for the last bite. We wanted to try Oysters à la Gino, a specialty at the inn, but oysters are not served out of season, and the month of our visit wasn't spelled with an *r*. Neither was it cranberry season when we were there, but the Cranberry Muffins, which I've since tested, are ones I'll bake again.

There is much to admire in the different rooms. Murals in the dining room were made from wallpaper samples used by manufacturers' salesmen 135 years ago. An enclosed Elizabethan staircase leads to the guest rooms; there are additional rooms in Robert Morris Sandaway Lodge and River Rooms, located half a block from the main inn. The rooms are decorated in a mix of antiques and reproductions to create a country-romantic feeling.

ROBERT MORRIS INN'S OYSTERS À LA GINO

2 tablespoons butter
1/3 cup all-purpose flour
1 tablespoon paprika
1/2 teaspoon monosodium
   glutamate (optional)
1/2 teaspoon garlic powder
1/2 teaspoon Chesapeake Bay–
   style seafood seasoning (if
   not available, add cayenne
   to other seafood seasoning)

1/2 teaspoon white pepper
1 cup milk
2 tablespoons Worcestershire
   sauce
2 tablespoons dry sherry
6 to 8 ounces (about 1 cup)
   cooked lump crabmeat
24 oysters on the half shell
6 slices bacon, cut into 4
   pieces each

Melt butter in a heavy pan over low heat. Mix in flour and dry seasonings. Stir in milk and Worcestershire sauce and whisk until smooth. Cook about 5 minutes until thickened, stirring constantly. Remove from heat and add sherry. Cool mixture for 20 minutes. Gently mix in crabmeat. Arrange oysters in a shallow baking pan and top each with a tablespoon of crab mixture. Place a piece of bacon on top of each. Bake in a 375-degree oven for 10 to 12 minutes or until bacon is crisp. Makes 6 to 8 appetizer servings.

ROBERT MORRIS INN'S CRANBERRY MUFFINS

1 cup sifted all-purpose flour
½ cup sugar
¾ teaspoon baking powder
¼ teaspoon baking soda
½ teaspoon salt
2 tablespoons butter
3 ounces orange juice

½ teaspoon orange peel,
  grated
1 egg, beaten
½ cup fresh cranberries,
  chopped coarse
¼ cup chopped nuts

Preheat oven to 350 degrees. Grease a 12-cup muffin tin. In a large mixing bowl, sift together dry ingredients. Cut in butter. In a separate bowl, combine juice, orange peel, and egg. Add to dry ingredients, mixing only enough to moisten. Fold in cranberries and nuts. Fill muffin cups about ²/₃ full with batter. Bake for 15 minutes. Cool and wrap overnight. Warm and serve next day. Yields 12 muffins.

ROBERT MORRIS INN'S SCALLOP CASSEROLE

6 tablespoons butter
1 cup onions, chopped
1 cup celery, chopped
1 tablespoon basil leaves
1 teaspoon poultry seasoning
1 teaspoon salt

½ teaspoon black pepper
½ teaspoon Old Bay seasoning
1 pound scallops
1 cup milk
1 tablespoon parsley, chopped
1½ cups breadcrumbs

Melt butter in a heavy skillet; set aside 2 tablespoons. Sauté onions and celery in remaining butter until tender. Add basil, poultry seasoning, salt, pepper, and Old Bay seasoning. Add scallops and sauté over medium heat approximately 5 minutes until tender, stirring constantly. Add milk and remove from heat. Pour into a medium-size bowl, sprinkle with parsley, and stir. Add 1 cup of breadcrumbs and mix well. Put into an 8- by 8-inch casserole dish or 4 individual casserole dishes. Mix remaining ½ cup breadcrumbs and 2 tablespoons melted butter, stir until moist, and sprinkle on top. Bake in a 350-degree oven for 7 minutes or until golden brown. Serves 4.

The Pasadena Inn

Route 329

ROYAL OAK

$\mathcal{W}$hen I arrived at The Pasadena Inn at Royal Oak, I was greeted by lilacs—big bunches of purple- and cream-colored blooms in clear glass—in the lobby facing the front door, on a table in the living room, and inside the white-brick fireplace in the dining room, my favorite

Dinner
6:00 P.M. until 9:00 P.M.
Monday through Saturday

For reservations
(suggested)
call (410) 745-5053

room in the mid-eighteenth-century mansion. There's an Old World look about the room, with wide, dark floorboards, dark-stained spindle-back chairs around tables covered with blue cloths laid over white ones, a built-in cabinet filled with blue and white dishes, and green vines entwining the freestanding chimney.

I had noticed the lilac bushes as Gordon and I drove onto the grounds on a Sunday afternoon. Royal Oak is about sixty miles from the Baltimore-Washington metropolitan area and a close neighbor of St. Michaels and Oxford. The Pasadena Inn, on the banks of Oak Creek, has guest cottages and hosts conferences on occasion; however, it is primarily known as a bed-and-breakfast country inn and restaurant specializing in "Creative American Cuisine."

The menu at The Pasadena changes weekly, but I have my ideal dinner selected for another visit. First, I'll have Focaccia—with cold Ratatouille, whipped butter, and hickory-smoked Tomato Cream Cheese—served with the House Salad of spinach with artichoke hearts, peppers, and Apple Walnut Vinaigrette. The entrée I want is Grilled Beef Tenderloin with Broccoli, Corn Soufflé, and Moroccan Vegetable Demi-Glace. I'll also order the Carmenet Moon Mountain Cabernet Sauvignon that the chef introduced us to.

We spent the night in one of the inn's dozen rooms, furnished with antiques; ours overlooked the dock, where light fare is served on certain nights and live entertainment is provided. A letter of instructions in our room gave us the rules of the house and information about where to find bicycles, badminton equipment, and boats, recreation which we unfortunately had to forgo. The letter was signed, "Sincerely, The Pasadena Family."

I thought of that the next morning when we talked to the chef over breakfast, which is served to inn guests. He referred to the staff as being like family. Our excellent meal was made more special by the fact that we had seen a painting called *Breakfast with Brian*. During a workshop held at The Pasadena Inn, a well-known artist painted French toast dusted with powdered sugar, accompanied by three sausage links, muffins, bright strawberries, cantaloupe, and grapes. The manager arranged to buy the painting as a gift for chef Brian Callahan before his marriage—and you may have guessed that we had the same breakfast with Brian that morning. I'd say they all were inspired—artist, manager, and chef.

THE PASADENA INN'S FOCACCIA

1 tablespoon dry active yeast
2 cups warm water
5 cups high-gluten bread flour
1 tablespoon garlic, chopped
1½ tablespoons rosemary, ground
1 tablespoon salt

2 teaspoons black pepper, ground
olive oil
2 pounds Italian plum tomatoes, sliced thin
½ cup fresh Romano cheese, grated
4 sprigs fresh rosemary

Dissolve yeast in warm water and set aside. Mix dry ingredients, make a "well," and pour yeast mixture into well. Mix by hand until blended. Transfer dough to floured table and knead 3 to 5 minutes. Place dough back into bowl, cover, and set in a warm spot until dough doubles in size. Transfer back to floured table and "punch down." Using a rolling pin, roll out to size of sheet pan (11 by 17 inches). Place on oiled sheet pan, brush with olive oil, and put in a warm spot until volume is almost doubled. Arrange tomatoes on top and bake in a 375-degree oven until brown. Top with Romano and fresh rosemary and let cool. Cut Focaccia into 2-inch squares. Can be warmed in oven if desired. Yields about 40 squares.

THE PASADENA INN'S JUMBO LUMP CRAB SALAD ON PORTOBELLO MUSHROOMS WITH RED PEPPER AIOLI

1 pound jumbo lump
   crabmeat
Vinaigrette (recipe below)
6 medium portobello mush-
   rooms, stemmed
1 red pepper, seeded
1 tablespoon olive oil

3 egg yolks
1 tablespoon white wine
½ cup olive oil
salt and pepper to taste
fresh herbs and edible flowers
   (optional)

Clean crab of all shells and mix into Vinaigrette; chill mixture for 1 hour. Roast mushrooms and red pepper in oven with 1 tablespoon of oil until mushrooms are tender and pepper skin is brown all over. Let pepper cool and remove skin. Purée pepper in blender with egg yolks and wine until smooth; add ½ cup oil slowly while blender is running. Add salt and pepper. Place crab salad in mushroom tops, top with a dollop of pepper mixture, and garnish with herbs and edible flowers if desired. Serves 6 as an appetizer.

Vinaigrette

2 tablespoons balsamic
   vinegar
5 tablespoons olive oil
1 tablespoon fresh basil,
   chopped fine

½ teaspoon garlic, chopped
½ teaspoon shallots, chopped
salt and pepper to taste

Combine ingredients until blended.

The Inn at Perry Cabin

308 Watkins Lane
ST. MICHAELS

$\mathcal{S}$t. Michaels is proud of its reputation as "the town that fooled the British," earned during the War of 1812, when townspeople hung lanterns in treetops, causing British cannons to overshoot the town. A navy veteran who served under Commodore Oliver Hazard Perry during the Battle of Lake Erie retired to St. Michaels in 1816 and designed a manor house with a north wing that resembled Perry's cabin on the flagship *Niagara*.

Now, the British have returned to St. Michaels. In 1989, Sir Bernard Ashley, co-founder of the

Breakfast
8:00 A.M. until 10:30 A.M.
Daily

Lunch
12:30 P.M. until 2:30 P.M.
Daily

Dinner
6:00 P.M. until 10:00 P.M.
Daily

For reservations
(recommended)
call (800) 722-2949
or (410) 745-2200

Laura Ashley Company, chose Perry Cabin as the location for the first of his Ashley House Hotels in America. The guest rooms, dining rooms, and conference room are in demand for "unique business retreats," but the appointments that most appealed to me had nothing to do with business. They were the furnishings—lovely antiques, paintings, flower arrangements, and English tea tables—in sitting rooms decorated with Laura Ashley fabrics and wallpaper.

Gordon and I were treated to lunch in a room where flowered cloths overlaid with white matched the flowered wallpaper, swags over windows, and curtains gathered over French doors. The service was as impeccable as the gold-band china; Gordon was surprised to find his napkin in its original folds when he returned to the table after a telephone call.

I agree with a quote from Sir Bernard Ashley: "If there are to be excitements, let them arrive at the dining table." The Soup of the Day, Squash Rosemary, was an exciting beginning. The hot purée, with buttery croutons in the center, was light green—zucchini, I guessed the squash was, and the waiter confirmed that with the chef. My entrée was Breast of Chicken stuffed with Zucchini, served on a Butternut Squash Purée with Baby Roasted Potatoes and Caramelized Baby Onions. Chef Mark Salter's recipe for Squash Soup appeared in the June 1995 issue of *Bon Appétit*. I should mention that I even write poetry about squash, my favorite vegetable.

After the War of 1812, Commodore Perry said, "We have met the British, and they are ours." We could say that, too.

THE INN AT PERRY CABIN'S CHICKEN RISOTTO

4 shallots, diced
2 tablespoons olive oil
1 clove garlic, chopped
4 boneless chicken breasts,
   cut into ½-inch cubes
oregano
small bunch of green aspara-
   gus, peeled
2 cups chicken stock or
   bouillon, preheated
1 cup long-grain rice, un-
   cooked
2 tablespoons celery, diced

½ cup garden peas, fresh or
   frozen
salt and freshly ground
   pepper to taste
2 tomatoes, diced
1 tablespoon fresh parsley,
   chopped
2 ounces unsalted butter,
   cubed
1 ounce Parmesan cheese,
   freshly grated
4 celery leaves, deep-fried

Gently cook shallots in olive oil. Add garlic and chicken. Sprinkle with oregano and combine to cook for a few minutes before adding rice. Simmer asparagus in chicken stock until just cooked. Remove asparagus and refresh quickly in cold water. Pour the stock onto the chicken and rice and simmer for 10 minutes before adding diced celery, peas, salt, and pepper. After approximately 12 minutes, the rice should have absorbed most of the stock. Cut the asparagus into smaller pieces. Add asparagus, tomatoes, and parsley to chicken mixture, finishing with butter and Parmesan. Garnish with celery leaves. Serves 4.

THE INN AT PERRY CABIN'S POTATO AND GOAT CHEESE TERRINE ON LEAF SPINACH

2 pounds Idaho potatoes,
  peeled and sliced thin
8 ounces unsalted butter,
  melted
salt and freshly ground black
  pepper to taste
4 ounces freshly grated
  Parmesan cheese
1 pound goat cheese

2 10-ounce packages fresh
  leaf spinach
freshly grated nutmeg
flour
olive oil
Black Olive, Tomato, and
  Shallot Dressing (recipe
  below)

Steam potatoes until just cooked. Brush with part of the butter, season with salt and pepper, and lightly brush the Parmesan. Line an oblong terrine with plastic wrap, then add slices of potato, starting around the perimeter and base. When half full, place the goat cheese in the terrine and pack potato slices over and around it. Continue to fill, then cover with plastic wrap and press, using heavy weights. Refrigerate for 4 hours before slicing.

Blanch the spinach for 1 minute, then refresh it and squeeze out any excess water. Sauté spinach in the remaining butter, seasoning with salt, pepper, and nutmeg. Remove the terrine from the refrigerator and cut crosswise into 8 slices, approximately ½ inch in width. Lightly flour and sear on both sides in a little olive oil; cook for 30 seconds on each side. Place spinach on plates, add terrine slices, and spoon Black Olive, Tomato, and Shallot Dressing over top. Serves 8.

Black Olive, Tomato, and Shallot Dressing

4 plum tomatoes, blanched,
  seeded, and diced
8 shallots, diced
2 ounces black olives, chopped
  rough

1 cup extra-virgin olive oil
3 tablespoons champagne
  vinegar
salt and pepper to taste

Mix tomatoes, shallots, and black olives with olive oil and champagne vinegar. Season with salt and pepper and serve over the warm terrine.

Harrison's Chesapeake House

End of Route 33
TILGHMAN ISLAND

$\mathcal{P}$oet William Stafford says, "The responsible sound of the lawnmower puts a net under the afternoon." I think the hum of ceiling fans on a screened porch provides the same sense of well-being, especially if the listener knows that Yeast Rolls are rising in the kitchen and fish are being caught nearby for supper.

To enter the screened porch and then the dining room at Harrison's Chesapeake House, guests walk past a sign that asks them to do four things: "Have a good time, remember us pleasantly, speak of us kindly and come back to see us again." The requests are easy to comply with, especially when part of the good time is spent rocking on the porch and talking with Mrs. Harrison — "Miss Alice" — whom Barry Goldwater, during his days as a United States senator, called "the world's greatest hostess."

She talks about the early 1900s (and before), when relatives came to the wharf by steamboat from Baltimore to stay in the family's guest rooms. Summer boarders came by horse and buggy, then by train, and drummers — salesmen — sometimes stayed overnight. Harrison's reputation for old-fashioned family-style cooking grew until the restaurant was regarded as a prime example of Eastern Shore country cuisine.

The "Buddy Plan" governs sportfishing at Harrison's. In addition to a night's lodging at the inn (the oldest part of which was built in 1856), it covers a fisherman's breakfast of Eggs, Bacon, and Pancakes at six o'clock, a day's fishing (tackle provided) on one of the twelve boats in Harrison's fleet, and a substantial box lunch of Fried Chicken, Crab Cakes, Sandwiches, Deviled Eggs, and Cake. If you're lucky, you'll have fish to take home — and Harrison's will clean and pack them.

For dinner, it makes sense to order the Catch of the Day. The day

Breakfast
6:00 A.M. until 11:00 A.M.
Daily

Lunch
11:30 A.M. until 4:30 P.M.
Daily

Dinner
Noon until 10:00 P.M.
Daily

Reservations are not necessary, but for information on seasonal closings, call (410) 886-2123 or (410) 886-2121

I visited, the catch was Sea Trout, a stronger-flavored fish than flounder, but milder than bluefish. My serving was thick and white and broiled in Lemon Butter.

Gordon wanted to taste the Crab Cakes that James Michener praises, and he was pleased to discover that a combination of Fried Chicken and Crab Cakes is the restaurant's specialty. A sixty-year-old tradition, it's called the Eastern Shore Dinner, and its reputation was upheld that night. We also enjoyed a variety of vegetables, and we learned why diners demand Miss Alice's Yeast Rolls, which she leaves the porch to prepare.

Her son, "Captain Buddy," or Levin Faulkner Harrison III, is the man in charge of Harrison's Chesapeake House and the sportfishing charter fleet. He carries on the tradition begun by the first Levin Faulkner Harrison's father, who left England to settle on Tilghman Island. Barry Goldwater thought Buddy's father was "the greatest ambassador of humanity I have ever met." The notes I made about Captain Buddy read, "Sandy-red hair and mustache, nice accent, likes to make people happy." Like father, like son, like six generations — because there is also a Bud and a little Buddy. No wonder theirs is called the "Buddy Plan."

HARRISON'S CHESAPEAKE HOUSE'S YEAST ROLLS

½ cup milk
3 tablespoons sugar
3 tablespoons shortening
1 teaspoon salt
½ cup cold water

1 package yeast
¼ cup warm water
1 egg, beaten
3 to 3½ cups all-purpose
flour

In a saucepan, combine milk, sugar, shortening, and salt. Heat almost to boiling. Remove from heat, add cold water, and set aside.

Dissolve yeast in warm water. Add egg and dissolved yeast to milk mixture. Mix in 3 cups of flour. Add extra flour as needed to make dough workable. Knead well until dough becomes elastic.

Put dough in a bowl, cover it with a cloth, and set it in a warm place. Let dough rise about 1½ hours, until it doubles in bulk.

To form cloverleaf rolls, pinch off small balls of dough; place 3 small balls in each cup of a lightly greased muffin tin and let rise again. Bake in a 400-degree oven for 15 minutes or until golden brown. Yields 2 dozen rolls.

HARRISON'S CHESAPEAKE HOUSE'S CRAB CAKES

1 tablespoon prepared mustard
1 tablespoon mayonnaise
salt and pepper to taste
1 egg, beaten
1 teaspoon fresh parsley, chopped

³/4 teaspoon Old Bay seasoning
¹/3 cup saltine cracker crumbs or fine breadcrumbs
1 pound backfin crabmeat
1 cup shortening

In a large bowl, mix all ingredients except crabmeat and shortening. Add crabmeat, handling carefully so as not to break the lumps. Shape crabmeat mixture into patties and fry in very hot shortening in a heavy skillet. Serves 4.

HARRISON'S CHESAPEAKE HOUSE'S BROILED SEA TROUT

²/3 cup butter
2 teaspoons lemon juice
salt and pepper to taste
1 medium onion, sliced

2 strips of bacon, cut in half
2 sea trout fillets
2 dashes paprika

Melt butter and simmer with lemon juice, salt, and pepper. Place 3 slices of onion and 2 half-strips of bacon on each fillet. Pour lemon butter over trout and cook under broiler until lightly browned. Sprinkle with paprika and serve immediately. Serves 2.

Kent Manor Inn and Restaurant

500 Kent Drive (Route 8)
KENT ISLAND, NEAR STEVENSVILLE

Although Kent Manor Inn sits on the tract that was granted to Thomas Wetherall in 1651, the first section of the manor house wasn't built until 1820. Dr. John Smyth began the home that was ultimately inherited by his grandson, Alexander Thompson. Thompson built onto the house, transforming it into the lovely showplace you see today, with its Italian marble fireplaces and eight-window cupola, from which he could view all 226 acres of his land.

The walls leading up the stairs to the cupola are lined with graffiti scribbled by guests who stayed here when this was the Brightworth Inn in 1898, Kent Hall in 1922, and later Pennyworth Farms. The inn fell into disrepair but was rescued and restored in 1986 by Frank G. Williams. It is now listed on the National Register of Historic Places.

Lunch
11:30 A.M. until 4:30 P.M.
Monday through Saturday

Dinner
4:30 P.M. until 9:30 P.M.
Monday through Thursday

4:30 P.M. until 10:00 P.M.
Friday and Saturday

2:00 P.M. until 8:00 P.M.
Sunday

Sunday Brunch
10:00 A.M. until 2:00 P.M.

For reservations
(requested)
call (410) 643-7716

I continued my tour with a visit to Thompson's former bedroom (Room 209). I'd been warned about its unusual odor. It's more than a little spooky that, after 150 years, the faint aroma of Thompson's pipe smoke remains despite a succession of cleaning crews. Scientists might argue that weather changes can activate certain odors, but what explanation can they give to the employees who believe they've seen Thompson's ghost riding a horse up the inn's driveway at night?

At lunch, I found that guests joke about, enjoy, and even request Room 209. And as I ate lunch on the enclosed back porch with a relaxing view of Thompson's Creek, I couldn't blame Thompson's spirit for wanting to be here. The atmosphere was one of lace cloths overlaying pink linen tablecloths, decorated baskets hanging from the beaded-board ceiling, and a crackling fire dancing beneath the black marble mantel in the parlor dining room.

I sampled the House Salad, created by owner Leslie Harper because she wanted a salad that would make a statement to her gourmet club. It combines artichoke hearts, hearts of palm, blue cheese, and bacon and is seasoned with a tangy Raspberry Vinaigrette. My entrée of Roast Quail stuffed with apples, raisins, and pine nuts quizzed my taste buds until I realized that its Apple Brandy Glaze was the secret that enhanced the quail's rich flavor. I also took a few bites of the Portobello Mushroom Sandwich, another inventive creation that will surprise those who think mushrooms are just for salads or entrées. The sandwich was served with a nice mix of Zucchini, Long-Neck Squash, and Tomatoes.

For dessert, I sampled the Chocolate Silk Pie and the Hazelnut Cheesecake. The cheesecake was rich, like the home's handsome decor, while the pie had a silklike subtlety that reminded me of the smoothness and comfort of things that have endured.

KENT MANOR INN AND RESTAURANT'S ROAST QUAIL

¼ cup pecans
2 tablespoons butter
1 small leek, diced
¼ medium onion, diced
1 stalk celery, diced
salt and pepper to taste
¾ teaspoon thyme
1 small Granny Smith apple,
   diced

¼ cup raisins
¼ teaspoon fresh nutmeg,
   grated
¼ teaspoon cloves, ground
4 quail
Apple Brandy Glaze (favorite
   recipe)

Toast pecans and set aside. Melt butter in a skillet and sauté leek, onion, and celery until transparent but still crisp. Season with salt, pepper, and thyme. Toss mixture with apple, raisins, pecans, nutmeg, and cloves.

Stuff quail with stuffing mixture and bake in a preheated 350-degree oven for 20 minutes. Ladle Apple Brandy Glaze over quail and cook an additional 5 to 10 minutes, spooning more glaze over birds at intervals. Serves 4.

KENT MANOR INN AND RESTAURANT'S PORTOBELLO MUSHROOM SANDWICH

1½ cups olive oil
6 tablespoons red wine vinegar
salt and pepper to taste
pinch of oregano
pinch of basil
pinch of parsley

pinch of thyme
4 portobello mushroom caps,
    cleaned
4 leaves of lettuce
4 slices of a large tomato
4 sandwich rolls

Combine oil and vinegar, mixing until incorporated. Add spices and stir until well mixed. Marinate mushrooms for 30 minutes in mixture, turning over caps. Place a mushroom cap, a lettuce leaf, and a slice of tomato on each sandwich roll. Serves 4.

KENT MANOR INN AND RESTAURANT'S HOUSE SALAD

3 cups artichokes, drained and
    chopped rough
1¾ cups hearts of palm,
    drained and chopped rough
3 strips bacon, cooked and
    crumbled
3 tablespoons blue cheese,
    crumbled

1½ tablespoons lemon juice
2½ tablespoons garlic, diced
2 green onions, diced
salt and pepper to taste
5 to 6 sprigs parsley, diced
2 heads romaine lettuce,
    cleaned and torn
Raspberry Vinaigrette
    (commercial)

In a large mixing bowl, combine all ingredients except lettuce and Raspberry Vinaigrette. Toss until incorporated. Place 10 equal scoops into beds of lettuce and pour vinaigrette over top. Serves 10.

P. Fairs

Bayard House Restaurant

11 Bohemia Street
CHESAPEAKE CITY

You can sit on the glass-enclosed porch or outside on the terrace of Bayard House Restaurant and watch large cargo ships and pleasure boats wind their way up and down the Chesapeake and Delaware Canal.

Construction of the canal began in 1804 beside the manor house that Samuel Bayard built in the 1780s. The canal was finally completed in 1829, when locks were built in order to float vessels from Chesapeake Bay to the Delaware River. The town that had been called Bohemia, for the Bohemia River, was then renamed Chesapeake City.

Shipping commerce made Chesapeake City bloom, and the town became a regular stop for a famous East Coast showboat named the *Adams Floating Theater*. Five years after the completion of the canal, Bayard's home was converted into Chick's Tavern and Inn. Sara Beaston took it over in 1845, and descendant Richard Bayard became its owner in 1858. It became known as Bayard House and was so popular that beds had to be rented in shifts.

Then, after the canal had enjoyed more than a hundred years of prosperity, the federal government purchased it and removed the locks. The town withered until 1948, when the current overhead bridge was built. Today, Chesapeake City is an attractive getaway destination for those who like to walk, shop, and eat in a historic setting.

Bayard House is now a restaurant with five dining rooms. I opted for a seat on the porch so I could watch the boats go by, but an evening favorite is the Red Room, decorated by Mrs. Richard Du Pont's amazing needlepoint creations. You'll see a needlepoint-framed mirror, valances, a wall hanging, and a mural-size piece in the entrance hall. I admire the work of this lady, who was the owner

Lunch
11:30 A.M. until 3:00 P.M.
Monday through Saturday

Noon until 2:00 P.M.
Sunday

Dinner
5:00 P.M. until 9:00 P.M.
Monday through Thursday

5:00 P.M. until 10:00 P.M.
Friday and Saturday

4:00 P.M. until 9:00 P.M.
Sunday

For reservations
call (410) 885-5040

of the famed racehorse Kelso and quite a few others. You'll also see paintings of her racehorses scattered throughout the restaurant.

You wouldn't expect a Mexican dish to be on the menu at a waterside restaurant, but Bayard House's Quesadilla Chesapeake is a different approach to traditional Mexican food. The chef combines fresh seafood with shiitake mushrooms, Anaheim peppers, and a splash of cheese, which blends the demarcation points of these ingredients. This Mexi-Maryland dish quickly became one of this old Texan's favorites. The restaurant's Chicken Pecan is volumes away from old-fashioned chicken salad, because you'll find *no* mayonnaise. Its big chunks of chicken, pepper, and spices seem to be held together by sheer will power, yet it coalesces in a way I wouldn't have thought possible until I made it at home. And it came with a smashing complement of fried oysters and tomatoes that did more than pretty up the plate.

For dessert, I had White Chocolate Whipped Mousse and Raspberries in a nest of Chocolate-Dipped Strawberries, which I found to be marshmallowy light and subtly flavored. It was truly difficult to leave this restaurant and seaside town that seemed like a step back in time.

BAYARD HOUSE RESTAURANT'S QUESADILLA CHESAPEAKE

1 to 2 tablespoons butter
4 medium Anaheim peppers, diced
2 tomatoes, diced
1 onion, diced
1 cup fresh cilantro, chopped
6 large shrimp, peeled and cleaned

6 ounces lump crabmeat, picked
4 medium shiitake mushrooms
1 cup cheddar or Monterey Jack cheese
2 8- to 10-inch flour tortillas
cooking spray
2 to 3 tablespoons sour cream

In a cast-iron skillet, melt butter and sauté peppers, tomatoes, and onions on medium-high heat until onions are transparent. Stir in cilantro for a few seconds and set mixture aside. Combine shrimp, crabmeat, mushrooms, and cheese. Place tortillas on a baking sheet sprayed with cooking spray. Put shrimp mixture in tortillas and fold tortillas in half. Bake at 350 degrees for 10 minutes. Remove Quesadillas carefully and place on serving plates. Top with pepper-tomato mixture and a dollop of sour cream. Serves 2.

BAYARD HOUSE RESTAURANT'S CHICKEN PECAN

2 chicken breasts
chicken stock to cover
1 medium red bell pepper,
    diced fine
2 tablespoons capers, drained
2 tablespoons shallots, minced

juice from half a lemon or
    more
$1/3$ cup pecans, chopped fine
2 heads Bibb lettuce
8 slices fresh pineapple
16 fresh strawberries

Place chicken and chicken stock in a saucepan over low heat; cook until done. Cool and cut chicken into ½-inch cubes. In a medium bowl, combine chicken, pepper, capers, shallots, lemon juice, and pecans. Cover and refrigerate for at least 30 minutes. Place chilled salad mixture in lettuce "cups" arranged on chilled salad plates. Garnish with pineapple slices and strawberries or other seasonal fruit. Serves 4.

Kitty Knight House

Route 213
GEORGETOWN

$\mathcal{D}$oes Kitty Knight still keep an eye on her house, built in 1755? Some say she still rocks in a chair here. If so, I'm sure she was delighted with the young women who roomed here during World War II while working in defense plants nearby. They were called "powder monkeys," which seems apropos at spunky Mistress Kitty Knight's place.

According to legend, when the British, led by Admiral George Cockburn, attacked Georgetown in 1813, Kitty Knight was waiting for them with a broom and buckets of scalding water. It's debatable whether she was a heroine or a traitor, since Admiral Cockburn dined at Kitty's that night, but only her house and the one next door were left standing when the British burned Georgetown. An alley that used to separate the two buildings now connects them with a parlor, where Kitty's mysterious rocking chair sits. A semitransparent mirror on the wall shows a faint, painted image of Kitty's face.

Reportedly, the house next door to Kitty's served as an Underground Railroad station. Now it is the Admiral Cockburn Tavern, where a disc jockey plays the latest tunes or a one- or two-piece band provides entertainment on Saturday nights. At other times, the jukebox and the cash register make the only music.

There are a dozen rooms for lodging at Kitty Knight House. Gordon and I slept in a light blue room facing the river. Our bed was iron; some are brass, and others are actually converted horse-drawn sleighs. The busiest months are July and August, when people vacation, often arriving by boat on the Sassafras River.

The restaurant serves Chesapeake seafood in a dining room with an early-American atmosphere, or in the gazebo bar, or outside on

Lunch
11:30 A.M. until 3:00 P.M.
Monday through Saturday

Dinner
5:00 P.M. until 9:00 P.M.
Monday through Thursday

5:00 P.M. until 10:00 P.M.
Friday and Saturday

Noon until 9:00 P.M.
Sunday

The restaurant is sometimes closed in winter.

For reservations
(suggested)
call (800) 404-8712
or (410) 648-5777

decks when the weather calls for it. Guests may have dinner in any part of the restaurant where there is a table. The chef stresses that Kitty Knight House is not just a "crab cakes and steak" restaurant, although the best-selling appetizer is Crab Cakes. Among the popular entrées are Lobster Ravioli and Blackened Tuna with Shrimp. Grilled fish specials are served regularly. Since Grilled Swordfish is a favorite of Gordon's, I asked for that recipe, as well as one for poached Salmon Beurre Blanc.

The sandwich menu is popular for lunch on the deck. It offers such things as Hamburgers made from meat ground at the restaurant, a Crab Melt (which is also on the children's menu), Hot Wings, and a Rib-Eye Steak Sandwich. I would like to sit on the deck sometime between May and September, when soft-shell crabs are in season, and enjoy that sandwich.

With no British in sight, I left Kitty Knight House, but not before I rocked for a minute in that chair.

KITTY KNIGHT HOUSE'S SALMON BEURRE BLANC

2 6- to 8-ounce Atlantic
   salmon fillets
2 cups water
¼ cup white wine
1 ounce lemon juice

Beurre Blanc Sauce (recipe
   below)
freshly chopped parsley or dill
   sprigs

Poach salmon in a large sauté pan with water, wine, and lemon juice. Liquid must cover salmon; add water if needed. Cover pan and slowly boil for 5 to 8 minutes. Remove salmon and serve with Beurre Blanc Sauce on top of or underneath fish. Garnish with parsley or dill. Serves 2.

Beurre Blanc Sauce

½ cup white wine
1 ounce lemon juice
dash of white pepper
½ cup heavy cream

¼ pound butter, room temperature
¼ teaspoon capers, chopped
pinch of dillweed
white pepper to taste

In a medium saucepan, combine wine, lemon juice, and dash of white pepper. Reduce to a very scant amount of liquid. Add cream and reduce to ¼ the original cream amount, until it is the consistency of thick pudding, stirring with a whisk over low heat. Add butter, whisking constantly until combined. Turn off heat just before butter has completely dissolved. Add capers, dillweed, and white pepper.

KITTY KNIGHT HOUSE'S GRILLED SWORDFISH WITH LEMON PEPPER

2 tablespoons butter
½ teaspoon lemon pepper

8-ounce swordfish steak

Melt butter and pour it into a plate. Add lemon pepper to butter. Press swordfish into mixture on plate, first one side and then the other. Grill or broil fish about 4 minutes per side. Serves 1.

KITTY KNIGHT HOUSE'S CRAB BISQUE

1 small onion
¼ cup sherry
2 tablespoons butter
¼ teaspoon curry powder
10-ounce can split pea soup
10-ounce can tomato soup

1 cup milk
¼ cup beef consommé
1 teaspoon Worcestershire
  sauce
¼ teaspoon Old Bay seasoning
¼ teaspoon paprika
4 ounces crabmeat

Purée the onion with sherry, then sauté the mixture in butter, adding curry. In a saucepan, combine the soups and milk with consommé and remaining seasonings. Add the mixture from the sauté pan and fold in the crabmeat. Heat thoroughly. Serves 4.

HOTEL IMPERIAL

P. Faris

Imperial Hotel

208 High Street
CHESTERTOWN

*D*uring the spring of 1774, Chestertown learned of the Boston Port Act, which closed Boston Harbor and demanded restitution for dumped tea. Shortly after that news, the British brigantine *Geddes*, also carrying tea, dropped anchor in Chestertown. Local residents had had enough of British "attitude." They passed a set of "Resolves" that forbade people to bring in, sell, or consume tea. The colonists then became "enemies to the liberties of America" when they boarded the *Geddes* and ceremoniously dumped the tea into the Chester River.

Maybe that's why proprietors Barbara and Bob Lavelle chose to install a Coffee Bar—rather than a tea bar—in the cellar of their elegant 1903 Victorian hotel. Neither a coffee bar nor a restaurant occurred to Wilbur Hubbard, who built the hotel to accommodate retail stores on the first floor and boarders on the second floor.

I stayed in a handsomely appointed room that opened onto a wide front balcony where breakfast is served. Guests can sip their fresh-squeezed orange juice and nibble on magical pastries while watching this quaint and friendly historic town come to life.

Locals and guests find the Coffee Bar's chummy cellar atmosphere a place to socialize and snack on Pastries and Italian Ices throughout the day. But for more substantial fare, they dine in either of the beautifully restored upstairs dining rooms.

I began my meal in the lounge beside a cozy fire in an old oak fireplace. I sampled chef Rodney Scruggs's Creole Crayfish Etouffée with fennel, peppers, and yellow tomatoes in a smoky Bourbon Sauce. If your palate needs waking up, this spicy appetizer will do it. The Portobello Mushrooms with Cilantro Pesto and Jalapeños could accomplish the same goal. Appetizer and entrée ingredients change fre-

Lunch
11:30 A.M. until 2:00 P.M.
Tuesday through Saturday

Dinner
5:30 P.M. until 8:30 P.M.
Tuesday through Thursday

5:30 P.M. until 9:30 P.M.
Friday and Saturday

Brunch
11:30 A.M. until 2:30 P.M.
Sunday

For reservations
(recommended)
call (410) 778-5000

quently, depending on the inspiration that assails this creative young chef, who likes to "have fun with food" and knows how to pull it off. Even salads are an event.

I switched to the Hunter Green Dining Room, where I had to sample more than one bite of my Arugula and Radicchio Blackberry Salad to decipher the different flavors. My next surprise was Brie with Apples and Walnuts. Brie lovers will especially enjoy this unusual preparation. Scruggs actually sautés the Brie before baking it, which, combined with sautéed apple wedges and walnuts, imparts a rich, yet brisk, taste.

Soup can sometimes be a meal. In this case, the Corn Bisque makes the meal. Scruggs says that local corn is the secret here, but this creamy soup is definitely one that, as a guest confided, "talks back to you."

The restaurant's signature dessert is pastry chef Lisa Scruggs's Chocolate Praline Triangle with Grand Marnier Sauce. One bite of this heavenly blend of chocolate and liqueur tells you why this talented lady is a frequent contributor to *Chocolatier* magazine.

I was too satiated to try Pork Loin Medallions or other Rodney Scruggs creations. I'll try those when I come back for one of his eight-course wine-tasting dinners, which bring food connoisseurs from Washington, Baltimore, and Annapolis.

IMPERIAL HOTEL'S CORN BISQUE

1 stick unsalted butter
1 medium Vidalia onion, chopped rough
4 large shallots, chopped
4 large cloves garlic, chopped
2 jalapeño peppers, seeded and chopped
12 ears fresh corn, shucked
1 pint chicken broth

1½ quarts heavy cream
salt and ground black pepper to taste
¼ to ½ teaspoon ground cumin
3 slices cooked bacon, crumbled
2 ounces Maryland crabmeat for garnish

Melt butter in a skillet over low heat and add onion, shallots, garlic, and jalapeños; cover. Sweat vegetables for 20 to 30 minutes. Cut corn kernels from cob and add to skillet. Stir and let cook for 3 to 4 minutes. Add chicken broth and bring mixture to a boil. Add cream and bring to a boil again. Reduce to simmer and let cook about 30 minutes. Place mixture into a blender and blend until almost smooth. Press bisque through a strainer with a rubber spatula. Season with salt, pepper, and cumin. Pour into 8 bowls and garnish with bacon and crabmeat. Serves 8.

IMPERIAL HOTEL'S BRIE WITH APPLES AND WALNUTS

½ cup clarified butter
4 sheets phyllo dough
6 ounces Brie cheese
2 Granny Smith apples,
    sliced in wedges

4 tablespoons walnuts
1 cup assorted greens
1 tablespoon walnut oil
salt and pepper to taste

Brush about an ounce of butter over 2 layers of phyllo dough. Place Brie on dough and cover with an additional 2 layers of butter-brushed dough. Wrap dough around Brie to enclose like an envelope. Place 2 ounces of butter in a skillet on medium-high heat and sauté Brie on both sides until golden brown. Place Brie on a cookie sheet in a preheated 350-degree oven for about 15 minutes. Sauté apple wedges and walnuts in remaining butter until crisp. Remove and drain on paper towel. Toss greens with oil, salt, and pepper. Place greens on individual plates, cut Brie into 4 servings, and place on greens. Sprinkle apple wedges and walnuts over Brie and garnish with additional uncooked apple wedges. Serves 4.

Harry Browne's

66 State Circle
ANNAPOLIS

red rose tied with an ominous black ribbon was delivered to Baltimore lawyer Jay Schwartz one day when he was eating lunch at Harry Browne's. At that time, Schwartz was lobbying in the Maryland General Assembly for a controversial bill. The "gift" of the rose upset him, since it was a *Godfather* symbol of death. Excitement spread to the newspapers, and Harry Browne's made headlines. Then it was discovered that several members of the assembly were just playing a joke on a friend.

Maryland legislators meet in the statehouse on the same hallowed ground where George Washington resigned his commission as commander in chief of the Continental Army in 1783. The statehouse sits on a hill across from Harry Browne's, so the restaurant is a convenient place for legislators to eat. The Jay Schwartz is a popular sandwich here; indeed, the crabmeat on an English muffin with cheese and tomatoes gets my vote.

Gordon and I didn't receive any red roses, but we did order a good red wine, Marquisat Beaujolais. We sat at the bar, embellished by an antique breakfront, and sampled Oysters Browne—oysters on the half shell topped with strips of ham and cheese and baked with just a dash of paprika. Owner Rusty Romo showed us a recipe used at the United States Naval Academy that calls for three pounds of paprika; the recipe was called "Crab Imperial for Four Thousand" (hungry midshipmen, that is).

Why would a man named Rusty Romo call a restaurant Harry Browne's? He named it for a favorite uncle. "Everybody has one . . . who always has a couple bucks to give you. You had one," Rusty

Lunch
11:00 A.M. until 3:00 P.M.
Monday through Saturday

Dinner
5:30 P.M. until 10:00 P.M.
Monday through Thursday

5:30 P.M. until 11:00 P.M.
Friday and Saturday

3:30 P.M. until 9:00 P.M.
Sundays

Sunday Brunch
10:00 A.M. until 3:00 P.M.

For reservations
(accepted)
call (410) 263-4332

said. (Yes, I had one. My uncle Clyde always wanted to be sure we had a nickel for a Coke.) Rusty's uncle was a builder whose passion was gourmet cooking. Uncle Harry would be pleased with both the construction and the menu of Harry Browne's.

The building has also served as a tannery, an inn, a bank, and a tailor's shop. Now, it is a restaurant with the air of a neighborhood bar, a 1920s speakeasy with a silhouetted *Great Gatsby*–era couple as its logo. Down the center of the room hang interesting light fixtures salvaged from the *Normandie*, which sank in 1944 and stayed underwater a year and a half in New York Harbor. The chandelier was in the ship's ballroom foyer, and the Zodiac lights hung in the first-class dining salon.

Rusty Romo says his uncle used to enter restaurants through the back door, because the food, the chef, and the kitchen were what interested him the most. If he could visit Harry Browne's today, he'd find plenty to interest him in his nephew's restaurant.

HARRY BROWNE'S JAY SCHWARTZ

1 English muffin
2 slices tomato

4 ounces crabmeat, picked
2 slices Monterey Jack cheese

Split and toast English muffin. Grill tomato slices. Stack crabmeat, tomato, and cheese on bottom half of muffin. Put under broiler until cheese melts, then top with other muffin half. Serves 1.

HARRY BROWNE'S OYSTERS BROWNE

1 dozen shucked fresh oysters
on the half shell
2 slices baked ham

6 ounces provolone cheese
dash of paprika
lemon wedges

Lay oysters in a baking dish. Cut ham in pieces of a size to fit over oysters and place a piece on each oyster. Divide the cheese into equal portions and top each ham piece with a half-moon slice of cheese. Sprinkle with paprika. Bake in a 350- to 375-degree oven for 4 to 5 minutes or until cheese browns. Serve 6 oysters with lemon wedges on each of 2 plates. Serves 2 as an appetizer.

HARRY BROWNE'S CRAB DIP

*1 pound cream cheese, soft-
  ened
2 teaspoons Tabasco sauce
1 cup half-and-half
1 teaspoon Worcestershire
  sauce*

*1 teaspoon garlic, crushed
3 tablespoons green onions,
  chopped
6 ounces crabmeat, picked
2 ounces cheddar cheese,
  grated
crackers or French bread*

Combine first 6 ingredients, mixing until smooth. Stir in crabmeat. Place in an ovenproof dish, sprinkle cheese on top, and bake at 375 degrees for 15 minutes or until bubbly. Serve with crackers or French bread. Serves 6 as an appetizer.

McGarvey's Saloon and Oyster Bar

8 Market Space
ANNAPOLIS

I would be drawn to McGarvey's Saloon by its looks alone. The narrow brick building has a symmetrical store-front that shows green cafe curtains hanging from brass railings. The number *8* (the saloon's street address) is stationed over the front door, and a green McGarvey's sign is mounted over that, centering neat architectural brackets. That's the way a saloon should look.

The building has functioned as a saloon since 1871 except during Prohibition, but the adjacent wooden building had never been an oyster bar until it became an addition to McGarvey's. As I stood on the sidewalk and talked to the owner and the chef, a neighboring restaurateur passed us and jokingly warned about me, "She pulled this on us yesterday!"

Hanging beside the bar is a plaque from members of The Annapolis Marching, Chowder, and Drinking Society expressing their sober appreciation to owner Mike Ashford for establishing McGarvey's Saloon and wishing him good luck. Obviously, the owner has been lucky, and he attributes that luck to an important location on the city dock, the "really good people" who work for him, a loyal local clientele, and traffic from the Intracoastal Waterway.

Mike Ashford welcomes Waterway travelers. He himself traveled for twenty years as an airline pilot. He took mental pictures of things he liked and noted the places that stood the test of time, such as Third Avenue bars in New York. He admired the oyster bar at Grand Central Station, with its individual steam heating pots. They influenced him when he turned an 1812 tobacco warehouse into McGarvey's Oyster Bar.

Lunching in the Oyster Bar, I found the interior bright and contemporary, with skylights, trees growing through grates in white tile squares, and sun patterns on wood. I tried Bratwurst and Smashed Potatoes, a special that was so popular at lunch that it was added to

---

Meals
11:30 A.M. until 1:00 A.M.
Daily

Bar
Open until 2:00 A.M.
Daily

Sunday Brunch
10:00 A.M. until 2:00 P.M.

Reservations not accepted
(410) 263-5700

the nightly special menu on Thursdays—"Locals Night." You can use this recipe at home with any good beer, but McGarvey's has its own Aviator Lager brewed to its specifications. It has its own root beer, too—"Old Hydraulic."

I also like the Monday special, Red Beans and Rice, which is served all day long. That dish is said to have a following akin to "the Super Bowl, male bonding, and puberty rituals." Hey, don't leave out the females; I used to live in New Orleans, the home of Red Beans and Rice.

McGarvey's has honored its good friend Walter Cronkite by naming an eight-ounce sirloin "Captain Cronkite's Steak." It is served with chili and chopped onions on the side. Mike Ashford, a sailor himself, says a sailors' rendezvous calls for ice-cold beer and a bowl of chili. After being denied such food during his days traveling, he wants to get back to basics.

MCGARVEY'S SALOON AND OYSTER BAR'S BRATWURST AND SMASHED POTATOES

48 ounces beer
1 large onion, chopped
1 teaspoon pepper
5 or 6 bay leaves
8 bratwursts (¼ pound each)
28-ounce can sauerkraut
½ teaspoon caraway seeds

½ cup applesauce
6 to 8 baking potatoes
3 tablespoons butter or
 margarine
¼ cup milk
salt and pepper to taste
2 cloves garlic, crushed

In a large pot, bring the beer, onion, pepper, and bay leaves to a boil. Add bratwursts and continue boiling to cook them fully but not split the casings. Remove bratwursts and discard the beer. Just before serving, grill bratwursts over an open flame for 2 to 4 minutes or place under a broiler to brown.

In the meantime, heat sauerkraut and add caraway seeds and applesauce. Peel and boil potatoes. When they are done, drain off the water and place potatoes in a large mixing bowl. Add butter, milk, salt, pepper, and garlic and smash (not mash) away. Potatoes should be lumpy, not smooth.

Present the dish by placing a bed of smashed potatoes on the bottom of each plate, followed by a layer of sauerkraut topped by 2 bratwursts. Serves 4.

MCGARVEY'S SALOON AND OYSTER BAR'S OYSTER CORN CHOWDER

1 medium onion, chopped
16-ounce can cream-style corn

1 pint milk
2 ounces ham, chopped fine
1 pint oysters with liquor

In a soup pot, combine first 4 ingredients and heat thoroughly. Add oysters and simmer for 5 minutes. Yields 6 cups.

MCGARVEY'S SALOON AND OYSTER BAR'S CAJUN CLUB SANDWICH

4 ounces breadcrumbs
1 teaspoon Cajun seasoning
8-ounce boneless chicken breast
1 tablespoon oil
2 strips bacon, fried crisp

2 thin slices provolone cheese, melted
2 slices white bread, toasted
shredded lettuce
1 slice tomato
mayonnaise

Combine breadcrumbs and Cajun seasoning. Bread chicken breast with this mixture and fry in oil until cooked. Top with bacon and melted cheese. Place on toasted bread with lettuce and tomato. Close top and cut 4 ways (club style). Serve with mayonnaise. Serves 1.

Middleton Tavern

2 Market Space
ANNAPOLIS

*I*t's fun sometimes to sit in a very old building and think about the famous people from history who have sat right where you are. Middleton Tavern is a good place for such thoughts.

If history recorded *you* as a famous person, what accounts would it give of your comings and goings? Thomas Jefferson's records note that in 1783 he paid Samuel Middleton for the privilege of riding the ferry from Annapolis to Rock Hall on the Eastern Shore. We know, then, that Thomas Jefferson was at Middleton Tavern, because the ferry was operated from the tavern building. That ferry offered all the more reason (besides food and lodging) for history's important people to visit Middleton Tavern. Tench Tilghman, for instance, used the ferry in carrying to Philadelphia the message of Cornwallis's surrender at Yorktown.

President James Monroe visited the tavern in 1818. At that time, it was owned by Mayor John Randall of Annapolis, who had been a distinguished Revolutionary War officer.

At one time, the building was a showplace, with gardens spreading from Prince George Street to the water. Now, without gardens, it stands at the corner of Market Space and Randall Street as a solid reminder of people who stopped at the tavern in pursuit of business and pleasure.

When Horatio Middleton acquired the tavern in 1750, he operated it as an inn for seafaring men. I thought of that as I ate a Middleton Tavern meal symbolic of traveling the high seas: Cuban Black Bean Soup and Lobster Luicci, Irish Coffee and Grand Marnier. It was beautifully served by the manager, who said he loved the extra touches—melted butter, orange slices, and parsley.

He expertly divided dishes for Gordon and me tableside so that we could sample Crab Middleton and Lobster Luicci, both served with toast points. The crab was a sensory delight—I could *see* the pimento and *taste* the lemon. I thought the Lobster Luicci was the best lob-

Meals
11:30 A.M. until Midnight
Monday through Friday
10:30 A.M. until Midnight
Saturday and Sunday
For reservations
(accepted for priority seating)
call (410) 263-3323

ster I'd every tasted—thanks, I think, to the tarragon butter baked on the lobster's breading.

Cuban Black Bean Soup I've had before, and I love the combination of rice underneath and chopped onions on top. Middleton Tavern serves cups of rice and onion on a plate to the side of the soup, so diners may add as much as they wish. This soup is not puréed; it's thick with whole black (or turtle) beans, simmered a long time with seasonings, green pepper, onion, and celery.

Who can resist Vanilla Ice Cream when it comes in a square chocolate cup filled also with wonderful strawberries, whipped cream, and slivered almonds? But we considered our real dessert to be the Irish Coffee. It tasted authentic; in fact, the owner of Middleton Tavern got the recipe in Ireland, from the Irish ambassador.

The crowning touch of the manager's "extras" was a sip of Grand Marnier that was 150 years old. That made *me* feel like a famous person.

MIDDLETON TAVERN'S CUBAN BLACK BEAN SOUP

1 pound black (or turtle) beans
¼ cup bacon grease
½ cup celery, chopped
½ cup onion, chopped
½ cup green pepper, chopped

½ teaspoon black pepper
1½ teaspoons salt
1 teaspoon cumin
1 teaspoon oregano leaves
1 cup rice
1 large onion, chopped

Place beans in hot water to cover. Soak for 2 hours, then parboil in the same water for 15 minutes. Pour off the water to remove acid. Rinse and cover beans with 2 quarts cold water. In a separate pan, heat bacon grease and sauté celery, onion, and green pepper. Add sautéed vegetables to beans. Add black pepper, salt, cumin, and oregano. Simmer, stirring occasionally, for 4 hours or until beans are tender. Serve cooked rice and chopped onion as accompaniments. Serves 8.

MIDDLETON TAVERN'S IRISH COFFEE

1 ounce Irish whiskey
1 ounce coffee liqueur
4 ounces coffee

1 ounce whipped cream
cinnamon sprinkles

Combine whiskey and liqueur with coffee in a glass. Place whipped cream on top and decorate with cinnamon sprinkles. Serves 1.

MIDDLETON TAVERN'S LOBSTER LUICCI

1 lobster tail
1 tablespoon oil
1 clove garlic, chopped
¼ cup Burgundy

1½ teaspoons dried tarragon
¼ cup butter
1 egg, beaten
½ cup breadcrumbs

Cut lobster tail out of shell. Crosscut tissues so they do not curl. In a skillet, heat oil and sauté garlic until opaque. Add Burgundy and tarragon and cook until Burgundy disappears. Add butter, stirring until it is melted and all flavors are incorporated. Dip lobster in egg, coat with breadcrumbs, and place in a baking dish. Pour tarragon butter over lobster. Bake in a 375-degree oven for 6 to 8 minutes. Serves 1.

Reynolds Tavern

7 Church Circle
ANNAPOLIS

$\mathcal{T}$ake a couple who studied urban planning at the University of Virginia and decided they wanted to run a restaurant. They saw an ad in the *Wall Street Journal* which led them to Annapolis, a model of town planning. Streets radiate from circles named Church and State. The historic building they became the proprietors of is an authentic tavern on Church Circle.

I wonder whether the Stallmans considered naming their restaurant The Beaver and Lac'd Hat, a name the tavern was known by in the mid-eighteenth century. At that time, William Reynolds rented rooms and operated an "ordinary which served hot and cold food and liquor to visitors," but he also conducted his hat business from the tavern, hence the picturesque name.

Lunch
11:30 A.M. until 2:00 P.M.
Monday through Friday

Dinner
6:00 P.M. until 9:00 P.M.
Monday through Thursday

6:00 P.M. until 10:00 P.M.
Friday and Saturday

5:30 P.M. until 8:30 P.M.
Sunday

For reservations
(suggested)
call (410) 626-0380

The Stallmans wanted to preserve the Reynolds name, in keeping with the building's history. In the 1930s, when a fuel company threatened to replace the tavern with a filling station, concerned Annapolitans arranged to convert the structure into a public library. When the library outgrew the building, the title was transferred to the National Trust for Historic Preservation, which in turn leased the structure to the Historic Annapolis Foundation. Now, the tavern has been restored to its eighteenth-century use—minus the hats.

William Reynolds would probably be impressed to see the original kitchen, now called the Colonial Kitchen, used for private parties; the Mary Reynolds Conference Room, on the third floor; the Franklin Street Pub, open till midnight; and the courtyard and gardens, a special place for wedding receptions.

Gordon and I were impressed by the restaurant, which specializes in creative cuisine. Blue woodwork, yellow cloths, and tall vases of daisies made a good first impression as Sandy Stallman greeted us. We were pleased with the number of appealing appetizers on the menu. The cold Peach and Raspberry Soup was painted with Melon Swirls. Poached Asparagus with Fruit Relish in Berry Vinaigrette was a visual delight. And Fricassee of Wild Mushrooms could take on anything. For our entrée, we chose Blackened Tuna with Tomatillo Salsa and Polenta. The Polenta slices were star-shaped, and four thin, green slices of Tomatillo garnished the plate.

There was no room at the inn when we were there, but sometime I'd like to stay overnight at Reynolds Tavern and sit in the garden. This time, we left through the Franklin Street Pub, where Gordon threw a dart that almost hit the bull's-eye.

REYNOLDS TAVERN'S POACHED ASPARAGUS WITH FRUIT RELISH IN BERRY VINAIGRETTE

24 fresh, tender asparagus spears

Berry Vinaigrette (recipe below)
Fruit Relish (recipe below)

Poach or steam asparagus until al dente, then chill. To serve, pour 1 or 2 ounces of Berry Vinaigrette on each of 4 plates. Put a mound of Fruit Relish in center of sauce and place 6 asparagus spears in a "tepee" pyramid over the relish. Serves 4.

Berry Vinaigrette

½ cup fresh or frozen raspberries, blueberries, blackberries, or strawberries

2 ounces white vinegar
2 ounces sugar
4 ounces vegetable or olive oil

Purée the fruit, strain, and add other ingredients.

Fruit Relish

1 small apple, diced fine
¼ fresh pineapple, diced fine
½ cup peaches, diced fine
2 ounces flaked coconut

1 tablespoon Rose's (sweetened) lime juice
grenadine to taste

Combine fruit with other ingredients and refrigerate.

REYNOLDS TAVERN'S PEACH AND RASPBERRY SOUP

½ teaspoon cinnamon
1 tablespoon peach schnapps
½ cup yogurt
fresh mint leaves

4 cups peaches
1 cup raspberries
5 tablespoons honey

Blend first 6 ingredients in a food processor until smooth. Chill. To serve, place in individual soup bowls, decorate with Melon Swirls on top of soup, and garnish with fresh mint leaves.

Melon Swirls

⅛ ripe honeydew melon
1 teaspoon melon liqueur

1 cup heavy cream

Blend ingredients until smooth. Put in squirt bottle to decorate.

REYNOLDS TAVERN'S FRICASSEE OF WILD MUSHROOMS

2 cups wild mushrooms
  (shiitake, crimini, oyster)
1 teaspoon shallots, chopped
  fine

3 tablespoons unsalted butter
¼ cup red wine or brandy
⅓ cup beef stock or consommé

Sauté mushrooms and shallots in butter on high heat. Deglaze with wine or brandy and cook until boiling. Add stock or consommé and cook until sauce is reduced to desired thickness. Serves 2.

Riordan's Saloon

26 Market Space
ANNAPOLIS

It was so crowded in Riordan's Saloon on one recent St. Patrick's Day that it took awhile to notice the Clydesdale horse, visiting Annapolis for the Spring Festival. It came in the back door and stood—head over the rail, other end out the door—drinking a bucket of green beer.

In the 1890s, when horses were a more common sight on the streets, Riordan's was a residence. Later, officers from visiting ships and the United States Naval Academy rented rooms on the second and third floors. The first floor was once a produce market that supplied ships in Severn-Annapolis Harbor. The store expanded to include drugstore items and then hardware before it became a clothing store.

Today, antique signs for cigars and whiskey are part of Riordan's decor, purchased by someone on the staff with an eye for auctions. Also on the wall is a caricature of Mike Riordan dressed to play ball for the Washington Bullets, before he traded that profession for the restaurant business.

Riordan's food is American, with an accent on sauces for seafood. One of the favorite Sunday brunch dishes is Seafood Mornay Randell, named for a chef. With its two good cheeses, scallops, crabmeat, and shrimp, it's easy to see why the dish is popular. The Barbecue Sauce on the saloon's Maryland Bar-B-Que Shrimp is also used on its Swordfish and Pineapple Kabobs.

I asked for the recipe for the veggie entrée that I enjoyed: a zucchini casserole, colorful with Eastern Shore cherry tomatoes and spiced with dillweed. It's called Brad's Choice, and I would choose it again, too.

Although seamen no longer live on the second floor of Riordan's, they can eat Maryland Lady Crab Cakes here by candlelight on Friday and Saturday nights. The first floor doesn't sell or dry-clean

Meals

11:00 A.M. until 1:00 A.M.
Monday through Saturday

10:00 A.M. until 1:00 A.M.
Sunday

Dinner on second floor
6:00 P.M. until Midnight
Friday and Saturday

For reservations
(not accepted for downstairs
dining but strongly
recommended for
second-floor dining)
call (410) 263-5449

clothes, as it once did. Today, you can get a Maryland Lady Crab Cake Sandwich or other quick meals downstairs.

If I were at Riordan's on St. Patrick's Day, I'd order Lamb Stew with Soda Bread and, of course, Corned Beef and Cabbage. I'd hate to overlook an Irish Hero, and I'd try the beer if it were the right shade of green. With enough of that, maybe I would see a Clydesdale horse.

RIORDAN'S SALOON'S MARYLAND BAR-B-QUE SHRIMP

Barbecue Sauce

1 medium onion, chopped fine	4 tablespoons brown sauce,
2 teaspoons butter	homemade or commercial
1¹/2 cups catsup	1¹/2 tablespoons vinegar
¹/3 cup water	³/4 teaspoon dry mustard
4 tablespoons Worcestershire	6 dashes Tabasco sauce
sauce	2 teaspoons tomato paste

In a large skillet, sauté onion in butter. Add remaining ingredients and simmer, covered, for 20 minutes.

36 large shrimp   18 strips bacon

Peel shrimp, leaving tail if desired. Wrap each shrimp in ½ strip of bacon. Place shrimp in a baking pan and bake in a 450-degree oven for 20 to 25 minutes or until bacon is brown. Drain off most of the bacon drippings and cover shrimp with sauce. Return pan to oven and allow sauce to heat for 3 to 5 minutes. Serves 6.

RIORDAN'S SALOON'S
BRAD'S CHOICE ZUCCHINI CASSEROLE

¼ pound butter
½ cup onions, chopped
2 fresh cloves garlic, crushed
3 to 4 medium zucchini, sliced
salt and pepper to taste

1 teaspoon dillweed
1 pint cherry tomatoes
8 ounces cheddar cheese, cubed
1 cup Italian-seasoned
    breadcrumbs

Heat butter in a skillet and sauté onions and garlic. Add zucchini, salt, pepper, and dillweed. Sauté for 5 minutes and reserve the liquid. Layer zucchini with tomatoes and cheese in a 3-quart buttered dish. Combine breadcrumbs with half the reserved liquid and sprinkle over casserole. Bake uncovered in a 350-degree oven for 25 minutes. Serves 8.

RIORDAN'S SALOON'S SEAFOOD MORNAY RANDELL

2 tablespoons butter
¼ cup flour
2 cups milk
2 tablespoons fresh Romano
    cheese, grated
4 ounces Gruyère cheese,
    grated

1 pound bay scallops
16 to 20 medium shrimp,
    peeled and deveined
1 cup white wine
½ pound lump crabmeat

Melt butter in a saucepan and add flour to make a roux. Add milk, stirring constantly. Just before mixture reaches boiling, reduce heat to medium. Add Romano, stirring constantly. When Romano is dissolved, add Gruyère, stirring constantly. Let simmer 5 to 10 minutes, stirring until thickened. While sauce simmers, poach scallops and shrimp in wine for 5 to 7 minutes. Drain wine and add sauce and crabmeat. Simmer for 2 to 4 minutes. Serves 4.

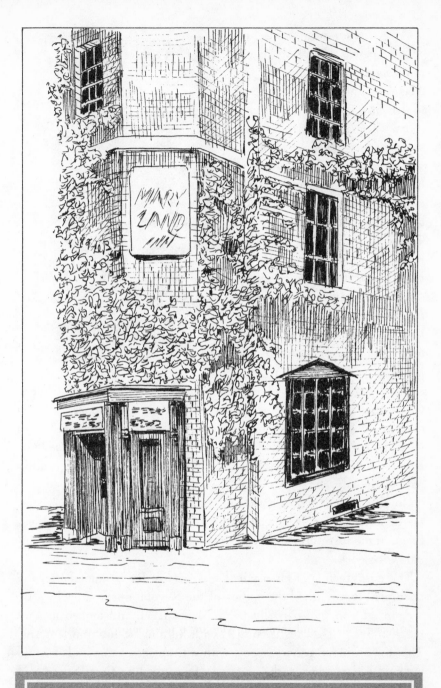

The Treaty of Paris Restaurant

Maryland Inn, Church Circle
ANNAPOLIS

An amusing thing happened when Bob Denver, of *Gilligan's Island* fame, stayed at Maryland Inn. It took five people to deliver a Club Sandwich to his room. They marched from the elevator with trays held high, one with a glass of water, another a napkin, then silverware, potato chips, and finally the sandwich he'd ordered from room service. These five were the day crew from The Treaty of Paris Restaurant. Frustrated because Denver dined downstairs only in the evening, when they couldn't meet him, they saw their chance and took it. And they got autographed pictures for their ingenuity.

Breakfast
7:00 A.M. until 10:45 A.M.
Daily

Lunch
11:30 A.M. until 3:00 P.M.
Daily

Dinner
6:00 P.M. until 10:00 P.M.
Sunday through Thursday

6:00 P.M. until 11:00 P.M.
Friday and Saturday

For reservations
(requested)
call (410) 263-2641

Maryland Inn stands on the choice, wedge-shaped lot on Church Circle that was laid out for the use of the town drummer, or town crier, in 1694, when the capital was moved to Annapolis from St. Mary's City. An earlier inn on this corner was advertised in a *Maryland Gazette* of the 1780s as "an elegant brick house in a dry and healthy part of the city."

Gordon and I spent a night on Maryland Inn's third floor. There, we experienced some of the luxury of the past—spacious quarters, fine antique furniture, and beautiful walnut banisters and other original woodwork.

There is a feeling of history in The Treaty of Paris, named after the document that marked the ending of the Revolutionary War. I sat by a deep-set window, partially below street level, and looked around the room at brick walls decorated with hunting scenes and lanterns. The low-ceilinged room is cozy, with a fireplace at one end. I could imagine a day when early-American favorites like Corn Sticks and Popovers—now also favorites at The Treaty of Paris—would have been cooked in that fireplace.

I soon got caught up in reading the wine list—interesting reading, with descriptions like "a white wine made from red grapes with a unique copper cast the same shade as the eyes of a black swan." We settled on a Byrd Gewurztraminer from Maryland and ordered Empanadas for an appetizer. The Spanish "little hats" are puff pastry filled with diced tenderloin of beef, spices, and the surprise of brandied raisins.

The Annapolitan Salad—artichoke hearts and shrimp on a bed of romaine and red leaf lettuce, covered with Green Goddess Dressing—was a treat to watch being prepared tableside. It proved to be even more of a treat to taste.

Eager to try the restaurant's number-one entrée, I ordered the Veal Oskar. This classic veal with crabmeat, white asparagus, and Béarnaise sauce deserves every bit of its fine reputation. Gordon tried the "Treaty of Paris" entrée—scallops, shrimp, lobster, oysters, and clams in wine, herbs, and cream.

After dividing a slice of Grand Marnier Cake, we made a pact to return to The Treaty of Paris.

THE TREATY OF PARIS RESTAURANT'S EMPANADAS

¼ cup raisins
¼ cup brandy
2 tablespoons olive oil
1½ pounds beef tenderloin
  tips, diced
5 tablespoons tomato paste
½ to ¾ teaspoon red pepper,
  crushed

½ teaspoon oregano
½ teaspoon basil
1 teaspoon salt
½ teaspoon pepper
1 to 2 eggs, well beaten
2 packages commercial puff
  pastry

Soak raisins in brandy until plump. In a skillet, heat the olive oil. Sauté beef, then add raisins and all other ingredients except egg and pastry. Mix well. Roll puff pastry as directed and cut into 48 three-inch rounds. On each of 24 rounds, place about 2 ounces of the meat mixture. Cover with the remaining rounds. Press edges of pastry together and brush with beaten egg to seal. Also brush tops with egg. Bake in a 325-degree oven for 25 to 30 minutes or until lightly browned. Yields 2 dozen Empanadas.

THE TREATY OF PARIS RESTAURANT'S VEAL OSKAR

11 to 12 ounces veal scaloppine
salt and pepper to taste
flour
2 tablespoons butter

4 ounces backfin crabmeat
8 spears white asparagus
4 tablespoons Béarnaise sauce
(mix or homemade)

Pound veal between sheets of wax paper (or roll marble rolling pin over meat) until it is very thin. Salt and pepper both sides and lightly dredge in flour. Melt butter in a skillet and sauté veal until pure white. Put veal on 2 plates and top each portion with 2 ounces of crabmeat, 4 spears of asparagus, and dollops of Béarnaise sauce. Broil until lightly browned. Serves 2.

THE TREATY OF PARIS RESTAURANT'S ANNAPOLITAN SALAD

1 bunch romaine lettuce
1 head red leaf lettuce
4 artichoke hearts

24 small to medium shrimp,
cooked
Green Goddess Dressing
(recipe below)

Arrange lettuces on salad plates. Quarter artichoke hearts and place 4 quarters and 6 shrimp on each of 4 plates. Cover with dollops of dressing. Serves 4.

Green Goddess Dressing

2 cups mayonnaise
½ bunch scallions, diced
1 tablespoon chives

1 tablespoon parsley, chopped
1 tablespoon tarragon leaves
3 anchovies, mashed

Combine ingredients thoroughly, mixing with a whisk. Yields 1 pint.

Note: This dressing keeps well in the refrigerator.

The Penwick House

Route 4

DUNKIRK

$\mathcal{W}$ant to know who is doing something about our national debt? The astute thinkers at The Penwick House. They discovered that importing foreign wines accounts for approximately 2 percent of the national debt. This fact, coupled with the belief that American vineyards are now producing some of the world's finest wines, inspired The Penwick House to develop an all-American wine list.

Having just glimpsed the Byrd Vineyards, nestled in the Catoctin Mountains, my daughter Daintry and I found our curiosity piqued. At The Penwick House, we satisfied that curiosity, sipping Byrd's 1981 Sauvignon Blanc as we looked out from a bay window onto an old-timey garden.

Lunch
11:30 A.M. until 2:00 P.M.
Tuesday through Saturday

Dinner
5:00 P.M. until 9:00 P.M.
Tuesday through Thursday

5:00 P.M. until 10:00 P.M.
Friday and Saturday

4:00 P.M. until 8:00 P.M.
Sunday

Sunday Brunch
10:30 A.M. until 2:30 P.M.

For reservations
(requested)
call (410) 257-7077

Often, I am asked to explain this "romance" I pursue with the past. It's difficult to convey the exact type of romance offered by a restaurant in a fine, old 1870 house. It has something to do with a garden with a gently curving walkway shaded by century-old trees, or wine served in an antique cut-glass carafe. Perhaps your ancestors lived in the manner of Dr. and Mrs. Chaney, who built The Penwick House. Perhaps, like me, you've read about this lifestyle and enjoy getting a taste of it. Whatever your background, it's fun to seek connections with the past.

While nibbling a tasty Mushroom Turnover filled with subtly seasoned sour cream, we wondered what it must have been like to come here for a piano lesson when the home was owned by "Miss Inez" and her husband, Jimmy Jones, who ran his country store out back. We decided that Miss Inez couldn't have been as stern as her former pupils claim, as the front banister is still loose from heavy use by students.

A lovely, crunchy Salad with Honey and Lemon Juice House Dressing was accompanied by a basket of Hot Popovers, Sweet Cornbread, and Bran Muffins so good that we almost considered not ordering entrées. But we knew that this was our last chance for Maryland seafood. I also knew that it was time for me to pare down on calories, so I selected the Fresh Bass-Striped Rockfish. The fish was so tender and the sauce so flavorful that each bite seemed to melt in my mouth. My ninety-eight-pound daughter, who haughtily laughs at calories, not only devoured every bite of a creamy seafood entrée called Our Made Dish, but allowed me only one tiny bite of the Amaretto Cheesecake.

THE PENWICK HOUSE'S MUSHROOM TURNOVER

2 sticks butter, softened
4 ounces cream cheese,
   softened
2 cups all-purpose flour
1 pound fresh mushrooms,
   chopped

2 tablespoons butter
½ teaspoon thyme
½ teaspoon garlic salt
½ teaspoon white pepper
½ teaspoon oregano
½ teaspoon sour cream
1 egg white, beaten

Mix 2 sticks butter and cream cheese together with wooden utensil. Add flour to mixture until completely incorporated. Cover bowl and refrigerate for 1 hour. Sauté mushrooms in 2 tablespoons butter until tender. Add thyme, garlic salt, white pepper, and oregano. Remove from heat and add sour cream. Mix well and set aside. Remove dough from refrigerator and let stand for 45 minutes. Roll out dough into oval shapes. Fill half of each oval with mushroom mixture. Fold dough over and press sides together to seal. Brush egg white over sealed edges. Place turnovers onto a greased flat pan and bake in a preheated 350-degree oven for 15 to 25 minutes until golden brown. Serves 4 to 6.

Crust

1½ cups graham cracker
crumbs

1 stick butter, melted
3 tablespoons sugar

Preheat oven to 425 degrees. Combine graham cracker crumbs, butter, and sugar. Grease a 9-inch springform pan. Press mixture into pan and ¾ inch up the sides. Bake about 5 minutes, remove from oven, and let cool.

Filling

1½ pounds cream cheese,
softened
1 cup sugar
3 eggs

½ cup butter, melted
1 ounce amaretto
1 cup whipped cream
1 pint fresh strawberries

In a mixing bowl, beat cream cheese with sugar until light and fluffy. Add eggs 1 at a time, beating to incorporate after each addition. Blend in butter and amaretto. Pour into cooled crust and bake at 350 degrees for 1 hour and 15 minutes. Remove, cool to room temperature, and refrigerate for at least 12 hours. Carefully loosen pan and remove cake. Top with whipped cream and berries. Yields 1 cake.

Blair Mansion Inn

7711 Eastern Avenue
SILVER SPRING

$\mathcal{W}$ hen I buy a wedding present, it is usually china. Never would I dream of giving newlyweds a gift that would entitle them to vote. But in 1880, Abner Shoemaker gave his niece Abigail and her husband, Charles Newman, a piece of land that promised this oppor-

Lunch
11:30 A.M. until 3:00 P.M.
Monday through Friday

For reservations
(recommended)
call (301) 588-1688

tunity. On the land was a grand Colonial-style mansion designed by famed architect Stanford White. Straddling the boundary between Washington, D.C., and the state of Maryland, the new home entitled the young couple to national voting privileges, which at that time were not afforded to residents of the District of Columbia.

Unfortunately, the ne'er-do-well husband gambled Abigail's dream home away in a matter of years. The mansion, which bordered the land of the Blair family for whom Blair House in Washington is named, subsequently acquired its neighbor's name.

Through the years, the mansion passed through many hands. It became a teahouse, then a boardinghouse, and it is even rumored to have been a house of prostitution. During the late 1930s, the home was renovated and turned into a hotel by Esterlene Bell.

Standing in the foyer, Rebecca Schenck, my daughter Daintry, and I listened to a 1910 Nickelodeon—America's first jukebox—and found it to be in terrific condition. The only difference is that it takes a dime to do what a nickel once did. I was also fascinated with the story surrounding a James & Bolmstorm piano that resided in the White House until Harry S. Truman's first administration. It seems that Truman had no luck convincing Congress to appropriate funds for White House repair until the leg of this piano crashed through the ceiling. Later, Mrs. Bell acquired the piano for her hotel.

As we lunched in the Library, we found that the stories were as bountiful and succulent as the food. One of the favorite rooms among guests is the State Room, with its mural of the Maryland State Capitol and ceiling fresco map of colonial Washington. Owner and chef Robert Zeender grew up in this family-operated restaurant. Even though the house is steeped in history, Zeender's divine culinary ability is more contemporary. We enjoyed fabulous, freshly baked Croissant appetizers stuffed with ham, cheese, and a variety of vegetables, each offering its own unique flavor. We also tried wonderfully crisp, sweet, hot Pineapple Fritters, which could easily be a dessert. For my entrée, I chose the Crab Imperial, a fresh, light, and delicately seasoned dish so different from the usual Crab Imperials I've tasted that I asked for the recipe.

Rebecca and I decided that you never get too old for peanut butter, especially when it is joined with chocolate and honey and melted inside a croissant. While we ate the whole thing, Daintry enjoyed the homemade Strawberry Italian Ice.

This was our first restaurant in Maryland, and I'm afraid we broke the one-bite sampling rule by eating every delicious bite that was put in front of us. We're not one bit sorry.

BLAIR MANSION INN'S CRAB IMPERIAL

*1 pound lump backfin
   crabmeat
1 egg yolk
6¹/₂ tablespoons mayonnaise*

*¹/₈ teaspoon Old Bay seasoning
¹/₂ teaspoon capers
3 egg whites*

Pick shells from crabmeat. Add egg yolk, 2 tablespoons mayonnaise, Old Bay seasoning, and capers and mix until well combined. With an electric mixer, beat egg whites until stiff; gently fold in remaining 4½ tablespoons mayonnaise and stir until mixed. Divide crabmeat mixture into 6 equal portions and place on a greased cookie sheet. Ladle egg white mixture evenly over top of crabmeat and cook in a 375-degree oven for 10 minutes. Serves 6.

BLAIR MANSION INN'S CROISSANT-PEANUT MELT

*2 tablespoons crunchy peanut
   butter
2 tablespoons clover honey*

*2 tablespoons chocolate chips
1 fresh bakery croissant*

Combine peanut butter, honey, and chocolate chips until well mixed. Split croissant almost in half and fill with mixture. Place croissant on a greased cookie sheet and bake at 350 degrees for 5 minutes. Serves 1.

BLAIR MANSION INN'S PINEAPPLE FRITTERS

3 eggs
1 cup milk
1 cup sugar
2 tablespoons vanilla
4 cups all-purpose flour

1½ tablespoons baking powder
1½ cups crushed pineapple, drained
1½ cups vegetable oil
1 cup powdered sugar

Combine first 4 ingredients and stir until mixture has a rough, wavy consistency. Add flour, baking powder, and drained pineapple and mix to incorporate. In a deep fryer, heat oil to 350 degrees. Drop well-rounded tablespoons of batter into hot oil. When fritters pop to surface, tap with a spoon until they turn over; cook other side to a golden brown. Remove, drain on paper towel, and keep warm until all batter is used. Roll fritters in powdered sugar. Yields about 40 fritters.

Note: Dip your spoon in an extra bowl of vegetable oil after putting each fritter into the deep fryer. This will help the next fritter slide easily from the spoon.

Mrs. K's Toll House

9201 Colesville Road
SILVER SPRING

$\mathcal{H}$ ave you ever gone out to eat and filled up on bread before your meal arrived? This won't happen at Mrs. K's, explained Mr. K (which is short for Kreuzberg), because "we don't serve bread until after the first course. When friends ask how you liked the Country Fried Chicken or Pork Roast with Dressing, we want you to be able to tell them."

Taking those words to heart, we nibbled sparingly when a lazy Susan chock-full of salad selec-

Lunch
11:45 A.M. until 2:30 P.M.
Tuesday through Saturday

Dinner
5:00 P.M. until 8:30 P.M.
Tuesday through Saturday

Noon until 8:00 P.M.
Sunday

For reservations
(recommended)
call (301) 589-3500

tions was set upon our table. Then we took a tour of this restaurant, which resembles an English country cottage complete with garden.

From the horse-and-buggy days of the early 1900s until World War I, the restaurant building was a tollhouse, where travelers had to stop and pay a toll for the use and maintenance of the road. Later, the old house became a teahouse, then a roadhouse, where America's beloved Kate Smith once sang.

In 1931, the Kreuzbergs bought the roadhouse and began serving "straight American food" amidst their antique collections. At Mrs. K's, you'll see Staffordshire blue pottery, pressed-glass plates that have been assembled into a plate-glass window, and an exquisite display of Nicholas Lutz glass. In the Dickens Lounge, you'll fall in love with the "mouse" clock, fashioned after the nursery rhyme "Hickory, Dickory, Dock." If arriving or departing at one o'clock, you'll see the mouse travel upward to one and fall down again.

We missed the mouse performance, but it was time for our meal, so we scurried back to our table in the garden room. Rebecca chose Baked Ham with Raisin Sauce. My one taste convinced me that the sauce was just sweet enough to enhance the moist, tender ham. I was lucky to get even a bit of Daintry's Old-Fashioned Pot Roast, as this "just-right rare" roast is hard to come by anymore. Since I've tried Country Fried Chicken in every other state, I ordered the Maryland variety, and I wasn't disappointed. It was crisp without a heavy batter, and was complemented by the surprise of Sherried Acorn Squash, with its tart citrus flavor.

Though controlling ourselves was difficult, we managed to spare room for dessert. The Slice Lemon Pie had a rich sweet-and-sour taste that I thought had gone out with my grandmother's baking. I was happy to find this elusive flavor—like so many secrets of old-fashioned culinary artistry—alive and well at Mrs. K's.

MRS. K'S TOLL HOUSE'S MACAROON PIE

3 egg whites
1 cup sugar
½ teaspoon baking powder

½ cup crushed pecans
12 crushed saltines
1 cup whipped cream

With an electric mixer, beat egg whites until peaks begin to form. Combine sugar with baking powder and add to egg white mixture gradually, beating until stiff. Fold in pecans and saltines carefully until blended. Spoon into a greased 8- or 9-inch pie tin and bake in a 350-degree oven for 25 minutes. Cool. Serve with whipped cream. Yields 1 pie.

MRS. K'S TOLL HOUSE'S SHERRIED ACORN SQUASH

2 acorn squash
salt to taste
4 tablespoons brown sugar

2 teaspoons orange peel,
* grated*
4 tablespoons dry sherry
2 tablespoons butter

Cut acorn squash in half and scoop out seeds. Sprinkle each half with salt. Place halves cut side down on a greased cookie sheet and bake in a 350-degree oven for 40 minutes. Turn halves cut side up and prick inside surface with a fork. Sprinkle each half with 1 tablespoon brown sugar, ½ teaspoon orange peel, and 1 tablespoon sherry; dot each half with ½ teaspoon butter. Bake 10 minutes longer. Serves 4.

MRS. K'S TOLL HOUSE'S SLICE LEMON PIE

Crust

3 cups plain flour
1 teaspoon salt
2 teaspoons sugar

1 cup shortening
5 to 6 teaspoons ice water

Sift dry ingredients together, mixing until combined. Cube shortening and add to dry ingredients a few cubes at a time. With 2 knives or a pastry blender, cut shortening into the dry ingredients until consistency is coarse and pebbly. Blend in 5 tablespoons ice water 1 tablespoon at a time, pressing dough against bowl until it masses. Remove from bowl and divide in half. With heels of palms, press each half out to form a 4- to 5-inch circle. Add more ice water if dough breaks apart. Lightly flour each circle. Cover each with waxed paper and refrigerate for 20 to 60 minutes. Remove 1 circle from refrigerator, place on a floured board, and roll out to fit into an 8-inch pie pan. Keep remaining dough chilled until ready to use.

Filling

3 lemons, peeled
4 medium eggs
2½ cups sugar
2 tablespoons melted butter

pinch of salt
½ cup water
dash of nutmeg

Remove lemon cores and slice lemons very thin, removing seeds; set aside. In a mixing bowl, slightly beat the eggs before adding sugar, butter, salt, water, and nutmeg. When well combined, stir in lemon slices. Pour mixture into piecrust. Roll out remaining crust and cover pie, pricking top for air vents. Bake in a 425-degree oven for 10 minutes, then reduce heat to 325 degrees and bake an additional 30 minutes. Yields 1 pie.

Normandie Farm

10710 Falls Road
POTOMAC

*J*ts name is spelled differ-
ently now; it used to be
Normandy Farms. A lounge is
where the kitchen used to be, at
the front of the house. And down
at the barn, there are no farm
animals for petting, which children used to admire when they
visited. But Normandie Farm is
full of memories for the people of
Potomac village and Washington,
and it's a matter of local pride to
come back to this 1931 restaurant
"where the tradition of hot golden
popovers and fine country cuisine
continues."

When Gordon and I were at
Normandie Farm for lunch, it
was the bitterly cold kind of day

Lunch
11:30 A.M. until 2:30 P.M.
Tuesday through Saturday

Dinner
6:00 P.M. until 10:00 P.M.
Tuesday through Saturday

5:00 P.M. until 9:00 P.M.
Sunday

Sunday Brunch
11:00 A.M. until 2:00 P.M.

For reservations
(requested)
call (301) 983-8838

when schools are out and pipes are burst and camaraderie is strong.
We found the great room, with a fire roaring at each end, nearly
vacant, but a sizable group of people sat companionably close on a
sun porch warmed by the sun and electric heaters.

Our table in front of the fire faced the Normandie coat of arms, a
fleur-de-lis banner, and copper pots hanging over the mantel. The
French Provincial room is full of folk art, from the rooster dishes
displayed in cabinets to the sayings and songs inscribed on dark beams
that stand out against the stuccoed walls. We tried out the old French
folk song *"Alouette"* as we sampled a house white wine, La Fleur.
When the chef appeared with the most popped-over muffins I've ever
seen, we sang to him. The Popovers, served with raspberry jam, were
a wonderful appetizer to introduce the specialty of the house, Filet
de Boeuf Wellington, served very pink and very tender. A layer of
mushroom and pâté underneath puff pastry did not overpower the
taste of tenderloin.

On the plate with the beef were two crisp Potato Balls, half a Tomato breaded and broiled, and a small bundle of String Beans "tied"
with a strip of bacon. The three accompaniments were just right in

color, taste, and size. I liked the crispness of the beans and plan to adopt the cooking method myself, although I realize that some Southerners would call it treason to cook green beans for no more than five minutes.

When a jazz trio or a pianist entertains in the lounge, the music flows into the dining room through a door marked overhead with more folk-song words: "*Frère Jacques, dormez-vous?*" A sign over a door in the lounge decorated with 1930s prints reads, "Rick's Café Americain"—a place lots of us would still like to visit. But even if we never get to that part of the world, we'll always have Normandie Farm.

NORMANDIE FARM'S GREEN BEANS

24 whole string beans
2 tablespoons butter
2 shallots, chopped

salt and white pepper to taste
1 tablespoon blanched almonds, sliced

Bring lightly salted water to a rapid boil. Add beans and cook for 5 minutes. Remove beans, plunge them briefly into ice water, remove them, and set them aside to drain. Melt butter in a skillet and lightly sauté beans with shallots. Add salt and white pepper. Add almonds and mix lightly. Serve 6 to a plate as a vegetable garnish; may be wrapped with slice of bacon or pimento. Serves 4.

Note: Beans may be boiled by the pound and stored in refrigerator for future sautéing.

NORMANDIE FARM'S FILET DE BOEUF WELLINGTON

2½-pound whole beef tenderloin, trimmed and peeled
2 ounces goose liver pâté
4 ounces fresh mushrooms, puréed in blender

¾ pound commercial puff pastry
1 egg
2 tablespoons water
4 ounces commercial madeira sauce

Sear tenderloin on all sides, leaving the center practically raw. Cool. Spread with liver pâté and purée of mushroom. Roll out pastry $3/16$ inch thick. Wrap pastry tightly around tenderloin, keeping seam on bottom. Fold ends under. Decorate with cutouts made from pastry trimmings. Beat egg with water to make egg wash and brush on surface of pastry. Place on a lightly oiled sheet pan. Bake in a 350-degree oven for 40 minutes or until pastry is done. If pastry browns too quickly, shield with foil. Cut in slices about ¾ inch thick. Serve 1 slice per portion with madeira sauce on the side. Serves 6.

NORMANDIE FARM'S POPOVERS

8 eggs

2 cups milk

1 teaspoon salt

1 teaspoon sugar

3 cups all-purpose flour

12 teaspoons oil

Mix eggs, milk, salt, and sugar. Add flour and mix for 1 minute; do not overmix. Put 1 teaspoon of oil in each cup of a popover pan or muffin tin and preheat pan for 10 minutes. Fill each cup ¾ full with batter. Bake for 15 minutes at 400 degrees. Reduce heat to 350 degrees and bake for 30 more minutes or until done. Yields 12 large popovers, or 24 small popovers if muffin tins are used.

Old Angler's Inn

10801 MacArthur Boulevard
POTOMAC

*O*riginally, Old Angler's was the hangout for local fishermen. A lot has changed about this romantic tavern since then. A lot has changed even since my last visit, when I pronounced the food *very good*. Now, with new chef Jeffrey Tomchek's talent for fusing unusual ingredients in his contemporary American cuisine, I pronounce his intriguing food *superb*.

Just as intriguing is Old Angler's history. George Washington designed the locks on the nearby canal. And during the Civil War, men from both the North and South were guests at the inn.

Lunch
Noon until 2:30 P.M.
Tuesday through Saturday

Dinner
6:00 P.M. until 10:30 P.M.
Tuesday through Friday

5:30 P.M. until 10:30 P.M.
Saturday

5:30 P.M. until 9:30 P.M.
Sunday

For reservations
(required)
call (301) 365-2425

Later, one of the "old anglers" was Teddy Roosevelt, who fished in the canal and no doubt lifted his glass at the tavern. That was after 1900, when the inn moved across the street to its present home, built around 1860. The inn, now only two hundred yards from the C & O Canal, lies near a former Algonquin trading post. Captain John Smith camped near here in 1608 during a canoe trip up the Potomac (then spelled Patauomeck).

In winter, soft sofas before a big stone fireplace in the downstairs lounge become the guests' comfort zone. They sit with a drink and ponder a menu that changes with the seasons. House-Smoked Salmon with Mascarpone Mousse and Petrossian Caviar, or Pot Pie of Wild Mushrooms? Pumpkin Chowder, or Asparagus with Caviar and Salmon? Venison with Mustard Sauce, or Salmon with Orange-Horseradish Crust? Duck, or Delmonico Steak? This early-spring day was too nippy for dining on the flagstone terrace that gives guests a blissful view of the woods above the C & O Canal, so I ordered and climbed the stairs to the French Country dining room.

My Pot Pie of Wild Mushrooms included a savory blend of carrots and celery root cooked in red wine, which embellished the taste without stealing credit from the shiitake mushrooms. The Pumpkin

Chowder was neither sweet nor bland, owing to smoked bacon and sweet corn that balanced its flavors. My Salmon with Orange-Horseradish Crust was the perfect example of successful fusion. It married flavors of salmon with subtle hints of horseradish placed atop wholesome lentils. I had to have that recipe, which was not hard to make.

Although the chocolate desserts sounded great, I've never been known to pass up a Crème Brûlée, and I wasn't sorry, either. Tomchek is a genius.

OLD ANGLER'S INN'S POT PIE OF WILD MUSHROOMS

1 cup wild mushrooms (shiitake, oyster, chanterelle, or black trumpet)
2 to 3 tablespoons unsalted butter
2 tablespoons shallots, chopped fine
1 tablespoon garlic, chopped fine
¼ cup carrots, cubed

¼ cup celery root, cubed
½ to 1 cup good-quality red wine
1 tablespoon flour
sea salt and black pepper to taste
2 to 3 sheets commercial puff pastry
1 beaten egg with 1 tablespoon water

Clean mushrooms, remove stems, and cut into bite-size pieces. Melt butter in a heavy skillet on medium-high heat and sauté mushrooms, shallots, garlic, carrots, and celery root for about 5 minutes. Reduce heat to simmer, add ½ cup of wine, and cook for 30 minutes, stirring occasionally. If needed, add more wine. Sprinkle flour over mixture and cook for an additional 3 minutes. Season with salt and pepper and place mixture in a 2-cup cassolette or 4 individual ramekins. Cut puff pastry to desired size to top cassolette or ramekins, brush with egg mixture, and bake according to package directions. Place cooked pastry atop mushroom mixture and finish in a 450-degree oven for 3 to 5 minutes. Serves 4.

*2½ pounds fresh salmon
fillets, skinned and deboned*

*sea salt and freshly ground
black pepper
Vinaigrette (see index)*

Wash salmon. Season with salt and pepper and refrigerate. Reserve Vinaigrette.

French-Style Lentils

*1 pound dark green lentils,
soaked
3 tablespoons carrots, cubed*

*3 tablespoons yellow onion,
cubed
sea salt and freshly ground
black pepper*

Rinse lentils thoroughly with cold water. Combine with carrots and onion in a saucepan. Cover with water and cook over medium heat about 30 minutes until lentils are al dente. Add more water if needed. When lentils are cooked, add salt and pepper to taste and set aside.

Orange-Horseradish Crust

*zest and juice of 1 orange
1½ tablespoons prepared
horseradish
½ cup breadcrumbs*

*1 stick unsalted butter, cut
into pats
2 tablespoons fresh dill,
minced*

Combine all ingredients in an electric mixer and beat until mixed. Roll into a ball, cover with wax paper, and chill before rolling out.

Roll out chilled crust between 2 layers of wax paper to the size of fillets. Cover salmon (including sides) with crust. Roast salmon in a 450-degree oven about 25 to 40 minutes until done. Heat lentils and add about 2 tablespoons of Vinaigrette to mixture. Place lentils on warm plates and top with salmon. Ladle Vinaigrette over salmon crust. Serves 4.

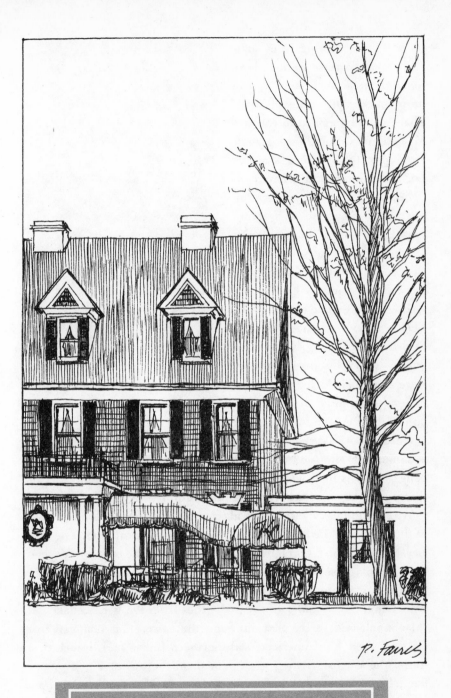

The King's Contrivance

10150 Shaker Drive
COLUMBIA

When suffering from some misfortune or accident, someone invariably says, "Something good will come of this." That's what happened to Richard Macgill, who injured his leg while hunting on the 370-acre farm that Lord Baltimore had granted his father in 1730. Richard got doubly lucky when he was found entangled in a barbed-wire fence—first, because his nurse was comely Rachel Clark, who nursed him back to health, and second, because she married him. This "accident" resulted in the rebuilding of Macgill's manor house, where his three children were born. The 1900s replacement was an even more prestigious Federal-style gray shingle mansion than the stone one built by his father, the Reverend James Macgill.

Lunch
11:30 A.M. until 2:00 P.M.
Monday through Friday

Dinner
5:30 P.M. until 9:00 P.M.
Monday through Friday

5:30 P.M. until 9:30 P.M.
Saturday

4:00 P.M. until 8:00 P.M.
Sunday

For reservations
(suggested)
call (410) 995-0500

Word has it that the spirit of a handsome woman in colonial dress is sometimes glimpsed upon the graceful, curving staircase at The King's Contrivance. Her identity remains a mystery, but odds are that it may be someone who lost her life in the original manor fire.

My springtime view from the glass-enclosed Veranda Dining Room of the lawn and the massive rhododendrons was a stunner. The light, airy, floral-accented porch became my favorite of the restaurant's seven dining rooms for lunch. I'll try the more formal Main Dining Room for a fall or winter dinner, when I'll have the famed Rack of Lamb with Dijon Sauce and 1 of the 174 wines from the wine cellar.

I was pleased to see that although the cuisine has changed from classical French to American with northern Italian and French overtones, the English Trifle has remained on the menu. For my appetizer, I wanted to try the fresh Tomato and Mozzarella with Basil, which seemed to cross just the right flavor boundaries. It had been awhile since I'd had Crab Louis, but I knew that it was among the restaurant's most-requested lunch salads. There are many Crab Louis imitations, but The King's Contrivance's combination of lump crabmeat with its extra-creamy dressing is something that seafood lovers are never going to stop asking for.

Sometimes, the anticipation of waiting for a dish can overwhelm it, but that didn't happen with the English Trifle, a lighter-than-light-tasting dessert. After a mere ten years, I finally got the restaurant to part with this fabulous recipe.

The dining here is such a cut above that it might well have been contrived by a king.

THE KING'S CONTRIVANCE'S CRAB LOUIS

*1-pound package baby
  spinach, washed*
*4 hard-boiled eggs, peeled and
  quartered*
*2 medium tomatoes, peeled
  and quartered*

*Louis Dressing (recipe
  below)*
*2 ripe avocados, peeled and
  halved*
*1½ pounds jumbo lump
  crabmeat, picked*

Clean and dry spinach and arrange on 4 plates with eggs and tomatoes. Drizzle a little Louis Dressing over top. Place an avocado half in the center of each plate and fill with crabmeat. Top with dressing. Serves 4.

Louis Dressing

1 cup mayonnaise
½ cup heavy cream, whipped
¼ cup chili sauce
2 tablespoons onion, grated

*2 tablespoons parsley,
  chopped*
dash of cayenne pepper

Combine ingredients in a medium bowl. Cover and refrigerate.

9-inch store-bought pound cake
2 ounces water
3 ounces sugar
4 ounces dry or golden sherry
2 10-ounce packages straw-
   berries, thawed and drained
12-ounce jar strawberry
   preserves

Vanilla Pastry Cream (recipe
   below)
½ cup raspberry preserves
½ cup walnuts, broken
½ pint heavy cream
2 tablespoons sugar

Slice cake into thirds and lay first slice in bottom of a 9- by 3½-inch glass bowl. Boil water with sugar until it becomes a simple syrup. Mix sherry with simple syrup and lightly soak cake slice. Combine strawberries with strawberry preserves and spread a layer over slice. Spoon a layer of Vanilla Pastry Cream over strawberry mixture; cover with a second cake slice and repeat, covering with a final cake slice. Cover top slice with strawberry mixture. Spread raspberry preserves over top and sprinkle with walnuts. Whip cream with sugar and place a dollop on each serving. Refrigerate. Serves 12 to 15.

Vanilla Pastry Cream

2 cups milk
4 tablespoons sugar
2 egg yolks
1 egg
2 tablespoons plus 2 teaspoons
   cornstarch

4 tablespoons sugar
2 tablespoons butter
1½ teaspoons vanilla extract
1 cup whipped cream

In a small saucepan, bring milk and 4 tablespoons sugar to a boil and cook to dissolve sugar. Remove from heat. Combine eggs with cornstarch and additional 4 tablespoons sugar. Temper egg mixture by slowly adding hot milk until mixture is combined. Return the mixture to heat and let boil, stirring constantly. When mixture has thickened, remove from heat. Stir in butter and vanilla. Cool in a covered shallow pan. Fold in whipped cream a tablespoon at a time.

Brass Elephant

924 North Charles Street
BALTIMORE

$\mathcal{H}$ave you ever watched a movie made in a foreign land and gotten so caught up in the mystery of an Indian temple or some wonderful castle that afterward you were surprised to awaken to reality? That is how I felt after our visit to the Brass Elephant for this revised edition. The interior dressing of this splendid old row house remains a beautiful blend of Eastern and European styles. The restaurant owes its grandeur to two gentlemen: Charles Morton Stuart, who built the house, and second owner George Wroth Knapp, a trader who embellished the lavish setting with exotic sculptures from his Chinese and Indian trade routes.

Seated at a brass-trimmed, rosewood-inlaid table, I sipped the house wine and understood why the Brass Elephant has won an award from *Wine Spectator* and the DiRora Award for the past three years. The wine is as enchanting as the room, which has stained-glass windows and a carved marble elephant in the corner.

If the wine doesn't clue you to the style of cuisine, the menu will. Randall Stahl is an innovative chef who has been at the Brass Elephant for over ten years. His longevity owes to the fact that he changes the prix fixe menu of three courses daily. Desserts change every week. While Stahl remains a devotee of northern Italian cuisine, you'll find other Continental offerings prepared with a French flair.

As a seafood lover, I couldn't pass up the chance to order the Paella Parellada, which has ingredients that make it deliciously distinctive. Rebecca, who chose the New York Sirloin Pizzaiola, agreed that her steak definitely had a highly original flavor.

I asked Stahl for his best dessert and was served Dried Fruit Com-

Lunch
11:30 A.M. until 2:00 P.M.
Monday through Friday

Prix Fixe Dinner
5:30 P.M. until 6:30 P.M.
Monday through Thursday

5:00 P.M. until 9:00 P.M.
Sunday

Dinner
5:30 P.M. until 9:30 P.M.
Monday through Thursday

5:30 P.M. until 11:00 P.M.
Friday and Saturday

For reservations
(recommended)
call (410) 547-8480

pote with Mascarpone and Brown Sugar Glaze. This very rich dish is reminiscent of the best fruitcake I've ever had. Normally, I'm not a dried-fruit fan, but Stahl's rendering made this a show-stopper. Afterward, I lingered over Cappuccino and was reluctant to leave the leisurely life of that opulent yesteryear.

BRASS ELEPHANT'S PAELLA PARELLADA

1/8 teaspoon saffron
2 tablespoons olive oil
1/2 cup onions, diced
2 tablespoons garlic, chopped
1/2 cup red peppers
1/2 cup chorizo sausage, cut bite-size
4 ounces chicken, chopped coarse
1/2 teaspoon paprika or cayenne
salt and pepper to taste
1/2 cup tomatoes, diced

2 tablespoons parsley, chopped
1 1/2 cups cooked rice
3 1/2 cups chicken stock (homemade or commercial)
4 cockle clams or other clams, cleaned
4 ounces ocean fish
4 mussels, cleaned
4 shrimp (16-20 size), cleaned and deveined
1/2 cup white wine
1/2 cup haricots verts *(baby French green beans)*

Toast saffron lightly, mash into a powder, and set aside. Heat oil on medium-high in a large skillet with a tight-fitting lid. Add onions, garlic, and red peppers and sauté until onions are transparent. Sauté chorizo sausage in a separate pan and drain well. Stir in chicken, sausage, paprika, salt, and pepper and sauté until chicken begins to brown. Reduce heat to simmer and quickly stir in tomatoes, parsley, and rice. Add chicken stock and saffron, stirring to combine. Lower heat and cover. When rice absorbs 2/3 of the stock (after about 20 minutes), add clams and cover for about 5 minutes. Stir in ocean fish, mussels, and shrimp. Re-cover and let simmer for 5 minutes. Add wine and *haricots verts*. Cook uncovered until seafood is done. Serves 2 to 3.

BRASS ELEPHANT'S DRIED FRUIT COMPOTE WITH MASCARPONE AND BROWN SUGAR GLAZE

Sugar Syrup

2 cups sugar
1 cup water
juice of 1 lemon
1/3 cup honey
2 cinnamon sticks
freshly ground black pepper to
   taste

4 pounds dried fruit (apricots,
   raisins, dates, cranberries,
   and cherries), chopped
2 tablespoons cornstarch
1 cup cold water

Place first 6 ingredients in a small saucepan and bring to a boil. Let cook until mixture reaches the syrup stage. Strain syrup into a large pot and stir in dried fruit. Simmer for 10 minutes. Dissolve cornstarch in water and stir into fruit mixture. Raise heat and stir until mixture reaches boiling; simmer until thickened.

Mascarpone and Brown Sugar Glaze

½ cup sugar
1 pound Mascarpone cheese,
   room temperature
2 tablespoons vanilla

2 tablespoons Grand Marnier
1 to 2 tablespoons brown
   sugar

Place white sugar and cheese in a bowl and beat until smooth; add vanilla and Grand Marnier.

To assemble, pour fruit mixture into a lightly greased ramekin or casserole and top with cheese mixture. Sprinkle with brown sugar and place under a broiler until sugar becomes glazed and bubbly. Serves 10 to 12.

Haussner's Restaurant, Inc.

3244 Eastern Avenue
BALTIMORE

"I hear from twenty reliable witnesses that you have married a most charming lady," H. L. Mencken wrote to William H. Haussner in 1935. Sixty years later, Maryland restaurateurs agree that Mrs. Frances Haussner is still a most charming lady. She presides over the restaurant her late husband established in 1926. The restaurant began in a build-

Meals
11:00 A.M. until 10:00 P.M.
Tuesday through Saturday

Reservations are not
accepted for dinner.

For group reservations
for lunch
call (410) 327-8365

ing across the street and then expanded to incorporate five dwellings on Eastern Avenue.

Gordon and I have often stopped in Baltimore just to enjoy a meal at Haussner's. I always take home a few postcards showing paintings from the Haussners' art collection, which shares the stage with the food.

"Masterpieces in art and dining" is the subheading on the menu and the postcards. Paintings that Mrs. Haussner bought at private auctions and estate sales cover almost every inch of wall space.

The museumlike second floor holds more art, including sections of the *Pantheon de la Guerre*, a life-size painting of six thousand heroes from World War I. The Haussners salvaged the painting and tried to find a home for it. No one place was able to handle the 45- by 402-foot work; however, a reconstructed portion is permanently mounted on a wall of the Liberty Memorial in Kansas City.

Then there is that other masterpiece: the dining. Looking at a list of thirty-five vegetables on the menu and not being able to narrow my favorites to fewer than five, I ordered a Vegetable Plate. My choices were Creamed Spinach (a specialty at Haussner's), Stewed Tomatoes, Candied Sweet Potatoes, Cauliflower, and Fried Eggplant. On other visits, I have selected from among the fine German entrées. This time, I obtained the recipe for one of my favorites, Sauerbraten, because to follow Haussner's recipe is to follow the leader. Just preparing the marinade of vinegar, Burgundy, lemon halves, and cinnamon sticks is a sensory experience.

The most popular dessert at Haussner's is Strawberry Pie, which is displayed with other delectable pastries in a takeout bakery department.

What do they call the cuisine besides German? The Haussners'
daughter says, "Mother calls it healthy."

HAUSSNER'S RESTAURANT, INC.'S, SAUERBRATEN

3½ cups Burgundy
1 quart vinegar
2½ cups sugar
12 lemons, halved and
  squeezed, juice reserved
1 pound chopped onions
½ cup mixed pickling spice

2 sticks cinnamon
4 pounds top sirloin butt
flour
1 teaspoon salt
½ teaspoon seasoning salt
½ pound gingersnap cookies,
  crushed
2 bay leaves

In a glass bowl or ceramic bowl (do not use metal), mix together
3 cups Burgundy, vinegar, 2 cups sugar, reserved lemon juice, lemon
halves, onions, pickling spice, and cinnamon. Add meat and let it
marinate in a cool place for a few days. Be sure the marinade completely covers the meat.

Remove the meat and place it in a roasting pan with about 4
cups of marinade. Roast in a 350-degree oven for 2 to 3 hours
until done. Remove meat to a platter and keep warm. Skim off
extra fat from pan and place it in a saucepan. Add enough flour to
make a smooth roux. Cook over low heat for 3 to 4 minutes.

Into the roux, strain pan juices and reserved marinade not cooked
with meat. Add remaining ½ cup Burgundy, remaining ½ cup sugar,
salt, seasoning salt, gingersnaps, and bay leaves. Whisk together
as mixture comes to a boil. Lower heat and simmer for about 20
minutes. If this gravy is too thick, add water; if too thin, simmer a
little longer to reduce. Slice meat and place on individual plates.
Pour gravy over meat and serve. Serves 8.

1½ cups sugar
½ teaspoon strawberry flavoring
½ teaspoon red food coloring
1½ cups boiling water
3 tablespoons cornstarch
   dissolved in ½ cup water
1 cup Pastry Cream (recipe
   below)

1 prebaked deep 9-inch pie
   shell
1½ pints fresh strawberries,
   washed and hulled (keep
   whole if small; cut in half
   lengthwise if large)
whipped cream for decorating
¼ cup toasted almonds, slivered

To make a glaze, add sugar, strawberry flavoring, and food coloring to boiling water. Add dissolved cornstarch and stir over medium-high heat until mixture thickens. Remove from stove and set aside. Prepare Pastry Cream and let it cool, then spread it in bottom of pie shell. Pour in ½ pint of strawberries, cover with ½ the water-sugar glaze, add remaining strawberries, and cover with remaining glaze. Decorate the edge with a circle of whipped cream and sprinkle with slivered almonds. Chill and serve. Yields 1 pie.

Pastry Cream

1 cup milk
3 egg yolks
¼ cup plus 2 tablespoons
   sugar

¼ cup all-purpose flour
1½ teaspoons vanilla
1 to 1½ tablespoons softened
   butter

Scald milk in a saucepan and set aside. In a bowl, whisk together the egg yolks and sugar until light in color and very thick, then beat in the flour. Pour the warm milk slowly into egg mixture and blend well. Pour mixture into saucepan and cook over low heat, stirring with a whisk until mixture comes to a boil. It will appear lumpy at first; keep whisking. Make sure mixture does not stick to bottom of pan and burn.

Remove from heat. Add vanilla and butter. Cover surface with buttered waxed paper so it does not form a skin. Allow to cool.

The Orchid French and Oriental Restaurant

419 North Charles Street

BALTIMORE

The orchid is a rare, exotic, and elegant flower that gives pleasure to those of discriminating taste. The same description applies to Baltimore's well-named Orchid Restaurant. Located in the heart of the city, this attractive three-story red-brick row house was built around 1870 and later became the residence of Emil and Emilie Fisher. Emil distinguished the family name when he became the agent of New York Dyeing and Printing—the forerunner of modern dry cleaning—in 1853. From the late 1930s to the early 1980s, a succession of businesses including an optician's office, a dress shop, and a hair salon made this their address before Singapore native Richard Wong transformed it into the award-winning restaurant it has become.

Lunch
11:30 A.M. until 2:30 P.M.
Tuesday through Friday

Dinner
5:00 P.M. until 10:30 P.M.
Tuesday through Thursday

4:00 P.M. until 9:30 P.M.
Friday and Saturday

For reservations
call (410) 837-0080

Today, the downstairs dining room's focal points are its large bay windows, its window seats, and its soft floral wallpaper. Each table is set with a rose-colored tablecloth accented by a spray of freshly cut baby orchids in a crystal vase.

For an appetizer, you can't go wrong with the Spicy Tuna. If this is your first visit, be sure to try the restaurant's signature dish, Fillet of Flounder Orchid. This dish has remained on the menu for over twelve years. Just one bite and you'll know why. Crisp almonds, ginger, and fresh pineapple combine with flounder covered with Beurre Blanc and Madeira Sauces. I also sampled the Canard Bigarade. This beautiful presentation, prepared from a boneless duckling, had a rich, hearty flavor. A gentleman who had watched me take a bite and scribble came over to tell me that this is the *best* restaurant in Baltimore.

Zagat and *Travel Holiday* magazines call The Orchid "excellent" and a "good value." After I sampled the Crème Caramel, I'd definitely put The Orchid in Baltimore's top five.

THE ORCHID FRENCH AND ORIENTAL RESTAURANT'S CANARD BIGARADE

¾ cup sugar   2 4-pound ducks
4 quarts water   salt and pepper
½ cup white vinegar

Lightly brown sugar in a large saucepan. Add water and vinegar carefully and bring to a boil. Place ducks in colanders and bathe them 2 to 3 times with boiling mixture. Salt and pepper cavities and let ducks dry in refrigerator for 6 hours. Preheat oven to 425 degrees and roast ducks for 15 minutes. Reduce heat to 350 degrees and roast for 30 minutes until crispy brown. Let ducks cool, then debone. Save bones for sauce.

Duck Sauce

¼ cup sugar   ½ stalk celery, chopped coarse
½ cup orange juice   pinch of fresh tarragon
1¾ cups water   duck bones
¼ cup tomato juice   1 teaspoon cornstarch
1 small onion, chopped coarse 3 teaspoons cold water
½ carrot, chopped coarse   juice of half a lemon

Melt sugar in a heavy saucepan until it liquefies. Add orange juice, water, tomato juice, vegetables, tarragon, and duck bones. Simmer for 30 minutes. Increase heat and reduce liquid to ½ cup. Strain sauce. Mix cornstarch with water and add to sauce; stir until it thickens. Bring to a boil for 2 minutes. Squeeze lemon juice into sauce.

Reheat ducks. Ladle sauce on plates and arrange ducks over sauce. Additional sauce may be added. Serves 4.

Flounder

¾ cup soybean oil
salt and pepper to taste
½ cup all-purpose flour
8 5-ounce flounder fillets
2 eggs, beaten
2½ tablespoons butter
5 tablespoons almonds, sliced

8 medium crystallized ginger
  pieces, julienned
3 tablespoons fresh pineapple,
  diced
Beurre Blanc Sauce (see
  index)
Madeira Sauce (recipe below)

Heat oil in a large skillet over medium heat. Lightly salt and pepper fillets and dredge in flour; shake off excess. Dip fillets in egg and fry until both sides are light brown. Reduce heat to very low and continue to cook for 5 to 7 minutes. In a separate saucepan, melt 2 tablespoons butter and brown almonds and ginger. Sauté pineapple in remaining butter in another pan. Place fillets on plates topped with almonds, ginger, and pineapple. Spoon Beurre Blanc Sauce over fillets and Madeira Sauce around sides. Serves 8.

Madeira Sauce

1 cup madeira wine
4 cups strong veal stock
1½ teaspoons chopped shallots

2 teaspoons cornstarch
¼ cup water
pinch of crushed pepper

In a small saucepan, combine wine, stock, and shallots over medium heat. Reduce mixture to 2½ cups. Combine cornstarch with water and add to sauce, stirring constantly. Add pepper and simmer over low heat for 15 minutes. Remove from heat and keep warm. Yields 2 cups.

Pierpoint Restaurant and Bar

1822 Aliceanna Street
BALTIMORE

The bright yellow sponged walls, green banquettes, and marble-topped tables at the Pierpoint Restaurant make you think that you're going to find Mediterranean food rather than Maryland dishes from the seventeenth and eighteenth centuries. Surprisingly, you'll find both at this tiny restaurant nestled into a 130-year-old Fells Point row house. "The colonial influence," says owner and chef Nancy Longo, "happened when I was asked to cater a picnic for the bicentennial celebration of Federal Hill." Using an August 1887 menu, Longo began her historical food research.

Although most eighteenth-century cooking techniques are no longer used, Longo found through experimentation that smoking meats and certain vegetables gives ingredients unique flavors, which made her want to use them in her restaurant. It's true that you can find Maryland Crab Cakes throughout the state, but Pierpoint is the only restaurant known to smoke them. Longo serves them and traditional Crab Cakes with Brussels Sprouts Slaw, an unusual and tasty dish in itself. Brussels sprouts have been popular since Maryland became known as one of the largest growers in the nation. And for those who don't love Brussels sprouts, this dish could change your mind. The combination of carrots and slaw dressing evokes a light, sweet taste that cuts the bitter bite of this much-maligned vegetable. The result is great, which is why Baltimoreans bring their out-of-town guests here to have authentic Maryland cuisine.

Research also revealed that Rabbit Sausage was an ancestral favorite. Longo makes it from scratch in the kitchen, along with many oyster, crab, tomato, and corn dishes that were once a part of colonial life. Since the era had heavy French and British influences, you'll

Lunch
11:30 A.M. until 2:30 P.M.
Tuesday through Friday

Dinner
5:00 P.M. until 10:00 P.M.
Tuesday through Thursday

5:30 P.M. until 10:30 P.M.
Friday and Saturday

4:00 P.M. until 9:00 P.M.
Sunday

Sunday Brunch
10:00 A.M. until 1:30 P.M.

For reservations
call (410) 675-2080

find liberal hints of sherry and brandy in Longo's Queen Corn Chowder and Maryland Eastern Shore Smoked Silver.

Depending on the season, desserts range from fresh Fig Tarts to Pecan Caramel Tarts, with Cantaloupe and Peach Sorbets and Ice Cream in the summer months.

The restaurant's wine and beer list favors microbreweries, with a heavy emphasis on regional and local wineries. My favorite was Eye of the Oriole's White Zinfandel, which was the ideal accompaniment to my Rabbit Sausage. The sausage was a surprise, too, as it was far lighter in taste than most sausages, yet delivered a surprising heartiness. The Rabbit Sausage is served with Spinach and a delicious Mustard Sauce. I coaxed the recipe out of this innovative young chef at her upbeat restaurant.

PIERPOINT RESTAURANT AND BAR'S RABBIT SAUSAGE WITH SPINACH AND MUSTARD SAUCE

1½ pounds rabbit, cleaned
from bone and ground
2 eggs
1 teaspoon garlic, chopped
1 teaspoon coriander, ground
½ teaspoon white pepper

1 teaspoon kosher salt
1½ teaspoons sage, ground
¼ pound bacon, cooked and
crumbled
2 pounds fresh spinach
Mustard Sauce (recipe below)

Place rabbit in a mixing bowl and add eggs, garlic, coriander, white pepper, salt, sage, and bacon. Mix ingredients until fully combined and shape into 6 patties about 2½ inches in size. Cover and refrigerate until needed. Cook patties in a heavy skillet over medium-low heat, turning frequently until done. Remove patties to drain on a paper towel; reserve drippings.

Clean spinach thoroughly in cold water. Remove stems and let spinach dry on paper towels. Add 2 ounces of Mustard Sauce to drippings in skillet. Raise heat to medium-high and add spinach, sautéing until it wilts. Place spinach and sausage on warm plates. Mustard Sauce may be drizzled over sausage. Serves 6.

Mustard Sauce

½ cup Dijon mustard
½ cup cider vinegar
1 teaspoon shallot, chopped
   fine
1 teaspoon garlic, chopped fine

2 teaspoons fresh thyme,
   chopped
1 pint olive oil
salt and pepper to taste

Mix mustard, vinegar, shallot, garlic, and thyme in a food processor or a mixing bowl. Add olive oil very slowly in a thin stream. Add salt and pepper. Yields over 1 pint.

PIERPOINT RESTAURANT AND BAR'S BRUSSELS SPROUTS SLAW

1 cup mayonnaise
¼ cup cider vinegar
2 to 3 tablespoons sugar
pinch of celery salt

2 tablespoons onion, grated
1 tablespoon lemon juice
1 carrot
1½ pounds Brussels sprouts

Combine mayonnaise with vinegar, sugar, salt, onion, and lemon juice and stir until blended. Grate carrot and rough-cut Brussels sprouts. Add to mixture, stirring thoroughly. Cover and refrigerate for a day. Serves 4 to 6.

Sabatino's

901 Fawn Street
BALTIMORE

*E*arly photographs of Little Italy in Baltimore show a distinctive feature at the intersection of Fawn and High Streets: a single post that appears to hold up the corner of a building. That building was the neighborhood candy store, which changed names as it changed owners— Granese's, Lou's, and Corky's.

Meals

11:30 A.M. until 3:00 A.M.
Daily

For reservations
(recommended anytime
and required on weekends)
call (410) 727-9414

Residents of the neighborhood point to the supporting post in pictures and say they remember it from childhood. At some time during modernization, the column was enclosed, but it was exposed again when the building became Sabatino's in 1955.

Row houses are practically synonymous with Baltimore, and Sabatino's is made up of three of them. The restaurant preserves the integrity of the neighborhood by keeping the three exteriors separate in colors, materials, stoops, and chimneys. The interiors, too, retain arched openings to show former divisions, so diners know whether they're sitting in the second or third house or in the former confectionery itself, where the restaurant first opened.

My favorite room is upstairs in the house farthest from the corner, where black-and-white photographs of relatives, friends, and former neighbors hang on the walls. The photo gallery makes an impressive memorial.

Rick Rotondo, whose grandfather is one of those pictured upstairs, spoke respectfully of the restaurant's founders, Joseph Canzani and Sabatino Lupereni. Rick, one of the present owners, says he knows 90 percent of the people who come to Sabatino's. He began meeting them when he was sixteen and became a "frontman," while his brother became a chef. Celebrity customers have included Frank Sinatra, Liberace, and Anthony Quinn, who came seven times during a two-week theater production of *Zorba the Greek*.

We enjoyed the house red wine, Marca Petri Pastoso. In a way, I'm sorry I tasted the Garlic Bread, an appetizer, because now I know what I missed by not getting the recipe. It is being marketed in stores, as is Sabatino's House Dressing. I can only say the mixture of garlic butter, oregano, red pepper, basil, and cheese is special.

The sauces on our entrées were very different, even though both contained sherry, lemon juice, and chicken broth. Gordon's Shrimp Scampi featured jumbo shrimp in a sauce that was spicy with garlic and other seasonings. My Veal Francese à la Sabatino's coating of egg batter and crumbs turned the sherry-flavored sauce a beautiful brown. Gordon and I divided the food; it was too good not to share.

I wanted a good, simple spaghetti sauce recipe from Little Italy, and I got it in Sabatino's Marinara Sauce. Haven't I heard that some people eat spaghetti for breakfast? I might return to Sabatino's to try that. It's open till three in the morning.

SABATINO'S VEAL FRANCESE À LA SABATINO

2 eggs, beaten
pinch of fresh parsley
pinch of salt
pinch of pepper
½ cup half-and-half
1½ cups or more breadcrumbs
1 to 1¼ pounds veal scaloppine

3 tablespoons butter
4 tablespoons oil
2 tablespoons flour
¾ cup sherry
juice of ¼ lemon
¾ cup chicken broth
4 slices lemon

Combine eggs, parsley, salt, pepper, and half-and-half to make batter. Place breadcrumbs in a separate bowl. Pound each slice of veal thin between layers of waxed paper. Dip in egg batter, then coat both sides with breadcrumbs, shaking off loose breading. In a heavy skillet, heat butter with oil and fry coated veal until it is golden brown. Remove veal and set aside on a warm platter. Add flour to pan and stir until brown. Add sherry and lemon juice, then chicken broth. Simmer for 3 minutes. Pour over fried veal and garnish with lemon slices. Serves 4.

SABATINO'S SPAGHETTI AND MARINARA SAUCE

2 teaspoons fresh garlic,
  crushed
4 tablespoons oil
4 cups whole tomatoes, peeled
2 teaspoons oregano
1 teaspoon basil
1 teaspoon red pepper, crushed

2 teaspoons fresh parsley,
  chopped
1 teaspoon monosodium
  glutamate (optional)
½ teaspoon salt
8 ounces spaghetti, cooked
  according to package
  directions

In a large saucepan or heavy skillet, fry garlic in oil until golden brown. Add tomatoes and spices and simmer over low heat for 20 minutes. Serve over spaghetti. Serves 4.

SABATINO'S SHRIMP SCAMPI

4 tablespoons oil
3 tablespoons butter
2 teaspoons fresh garlic,
  crushed
20 jumbo shrimp
½ teaspoon red pepper, crushed
1 teaspoon oregano

½ teaspoon salt
½ teaspoon monosodium
  glutamate (optional)
2 tablespoons flour
½ cup sherry
juice of ¼ lemon
¾ cup chicken broth

In a heavy skillet, heat oil and butter; add garlic and sauté until slightly brown. Add shrimp and cook until firm. Add spices and flour, stirring well. Add sherry and lemon juice, then chicken broth. Simmer over low heat for 10 minutes. Place 5 shrimp on each of 4 plates and cover with sauce. Serves 4.

Fiori

100 Painters Mill Road
OWINGS MILL

$\mathcal{H}$ ow would you like to grow up having the job of lookout to protect against Indians? Apparently, that was the job of millionaire Samuel Owings's children in this 1767 Federal-style mansion. The space where a window was inserted in the chimney is only large enough for a child. It sounds like a dull job, but the guard could be changed often, because Owings had twelve children.

When modern families outgrow their surroundings, they generally move to a larger home. In Owings's day, many houses took on a crazy-quilt appearance, but in his "U.L.M." House (named with the initials of the upper, lower, and middle mills of the Owings empire), the only evidence of enlargement is the soft texture of interior brick walls that have never weathered the elements.

Lunch
11:30 A.M. until 2:30 P.M.
Monday through Friday

Dinner
5:30 P.M. until 9:00 P.M.
Monday through Saturday

4:00 P.M. until 8:00 P.M.
Sunday

The Stone Cellar Lounge
stays open until 11:00 P.M.
on weekends.

For reservations
(recommended)
call (410) 363-3131

The restaurant continues to bloom with springtime pastels even though it has changed both its name and its style of cuisine. Formerly the Country Fare Inn, Fiori now serves classic Italian cuisine, with a few regional American dishes to add interest for folks who want to try out Maryland favorites. The day that I visited this comfortable restaurant, two separate parties were in progress. A group of business people was celebrating in one intimate dining room beside the large foyer and a group of ladies was having lunch and playing bridge in the opposite dining room. This is one of the beauties of old homes. Different activities can occur simultaneously without disturbing each other.

I dined in the rustic back dining room near an attractive hearth. I began with a bowl of Minestrone Soup. The variety of ingredients in this soup comes together with a nice garnish of Parmesan cheese. My salad was an attractive combination of spinach and fresh shrimp garnished with pine nuts and croutons, but the Dijon Mustard Dressing lent a snappy authority that went well with a serving of Polenta. Since fellow diners told me that this restaurant is known for its Roquefort Dressing, I sampled a few bites on a tossed salad. True to their words, the dressing is creamy but still delivers the sting that only real Roquefort can present.

You don't come to Maryland without ordering a Crab Cake. And I've found that each restaurant's offering is a little different from every other restaurant's. Fiori uses equal amounts of lump and backfin crabmeat, which produces a cake with great crab definition. This was accompanied by the restaurant's specially seasoned Curly Fries. If I had a larger appetite, I would have ordered either the Rigatoni Fiori, which is pasta topped with bacon, onions, mushrooms, and spinach in a rich Marinara Sauce, or the Fiori Sandwich, which combines prosciutto, Genoa salami, capocollo, and provolone grilled with a tomato on an Italian roll.

The dinner menu features a fairly equal number of Italian and American entrées, but locals advise either the Lasagna, which is made with fresh pasta layered with Italian sausage and cheeses and topped with Bolognese and provolone, or the Meat Loaf, which is topped with Mushroom Espagnole Sauce. Or you can order a good New York Strip or Grilled Chicken.

Fiori has a wide selection of Continental wines, with a heavy emphasis on Italian vintages. I declined, as I was traveling, comforting myself instead with generous samples of two desserts. Most guests seem to prefer the Chocolate Cake Fiori, a very rich, chocolaty concoction, but my interest was swayed by the Chocolate Sabayon, which is lighter, but no less appealing. Served in a dessert glass, the chocolate and whipped cream intermingle with the surprise introduction of raspberries. This was a recipe I had to have before leaving this cozy restaurant.

FIORI'S CHOCOLATE SABAYON

1 cup heavy whipping cream
3 egg yolks
2 ounces sugar
3 tablespoons Cointreau
1 teaspoon plain gelatin

¼ cup hot water
2 ounces semisweet chocolate,
 melted
6 teaspoons raspberry preserves

Whip cream to soft peaks and set aside in refrigerator. In a separate mixing bowl, whisk together egg yolks, sugar, and Cointreau. Place in a double boiler over hot—not boiling—water and whisk, turning pan continually until candy thermometer reaches 110 degrees. Remove from heat immediately and continue to whip until mixture reaches room temperature. Combine gelatin and hot water and stir until absorbed. Whisk gelatin mixture into egg mixture and stir until well mixed. Add chocolate, whisking until combined. Carefully fold in whipped cream, being careful not to break down cream. Line six 6-ounce dessert glasses with raspberry preserves and fill glasses equally with chocolate mixture. Refrigerate. Serves 6.

FIORI'S ROQUEFORT DRESSING

1 cup sour cream
1 to 2 tablespoons mayon-
 naise
1 ounce half-and-half
½ teaspoon garlic, crushed

¼ teaspoon salt
pinch of cayenne pepper
white pepper to taste
4 ounces Roquefort cheese

Combine sour cream and mayonnaise in a mixer. Slowly add half-and-half until well mixed. Add garlic, salt, cayenne pepper, and white pepper, mixing until all ingredients are incorporated. Stir in cheese; cover and refrigerate. Yields over 1 cup.

Milton Inn

14833 York Road
SPARKS

$\mathcal{W}$ould you have turned Clark Gable from your door, even if he was with Carole Lombard? Neither would I, but that was the actor's reception at the Milton Inn when it was the private home of Polly Leiter. According to the story, the Gables were intrigued by Maryland antiques, and one of Leiter's friends assured Hollywood's golden couple that they would be welcome at Leiter's antique-filled home. Unfortunately, no one told Polly Leiter, who had instructed her butler to admit no callers while she was taking a nap to relieve a champagne hangover. Bad timing, or what?

Dinner
5:30 P.M. until 9:30 P.M.
Monday through Saturday

5:00 P.M. until 8:00 P.M.
Sunday

For reservations
(recommended)
call (410) 771-4366

Our timing was much better—we arrived at dinner. The side entrance led us through the cobblestone-floored Hearth Room, which was the kitchen in the house's early days. Hot meals were prepared at the room's enormous fireplace for the coachmen who drove Quakers down the road to monthly religious services at the New Gunpowder Meeting House. The fieldstone residence, which is the oldest building in Baltimore County, is thought to have been built by a Quaker named Thom in 1740.

After its use as a coachmen's inn, the ivy-covered structure was transformed in 1847 into a school for wealthy Maryland boys, the most notorious of whom was John Wilkes Booth. What did that young man learn here? We pondered that question while seated upstairs in the cozy, colonial York Room. The room's pastel walls feature celebrated Maryland artist John Sills, and you can't imagine that it once functioned as a classroom.

Rebecca and I sampled Oysters on the Half Shell, which offered a real zing when coupled with a tangy Herb Vinaigrette accented with shaved horseradish. Since our previous visit, the inn has added apple to the watercress and hearts of palm in its recipe for Eleanora Salad, so I tried this crunchier offering and found the addition perfect. Fortunately, Soft-Shell Crabs were in season, so we shared this delicacy, made even more special by its rich Beurre Blanc Sauce, which didn't mask the fresh crab taste. It would be hard to overshadow the famed Maryland Crab Cake, but the inn's Lobster, Crab, and Corn Cake certainly belongs in the winner's box, with its creamy, distinctive seafood variety.

Between bites, we learned that the former boys' school was named after the poet John Milton, author of *Paradise Lost*. The curriculum included Greek, Latin, and English classes—hardly fodder for budding assassins, so Booth was no doubt influenced elsewhere.

MILTON INN'S LOBSTER, CRAB, AND CORN CAKE

8 ounces fresh fish fillet (sea bass or fluke), very cold
1 clove garlic, chopped
1 teaspoon Old Bay seasoning
½ teaspoon Pommery mustard
½ teaspoon salt
½ teaspoon white pepper
1 egg, cold
1 cup heavy cream
1 pound jumbo lump crabmeat

8 ounces lobster, cooked and diced
8 ounces sweet corn kernels, cooked
1 smoked chili pepper, chopped fine
1½ cups breadcrumbs
2 to 3 tablespoons clarified butter
Beurre Blanc Sauce (recipe follows)

In a food processor, combine fish, garlic, Old Bay seasoning, mustard, salt, and pepper. Process until mixture is smooth. Add egg and mix until fully combined. Add cream through the feed tube and process until emulsified. Mixture should look smooth and shiny. Remove mixture from processor and place in a large mixing bowl. Add crab, lobster, corn, and chili pepper. Mix together without breaking crab lumps. Remove from bowl and form into 4-ounce patties. Coat liberally with breadcrumbs on both sides. Fry in clarified butter until golden on both sides. Set aside and keep warm. Ladle Beurre Blanc Sauce generously over cakes. Serves 6.

Beurre Blanc Sauce

4 shallots, sliced
6 ounces white wine
2 tablespoons heavy cream

12 ounces unsalted butter,
    softened and cut in pieces
juice of half a lemon
salt to taste

Place shallots in a small saucepan and pour wine over them. Cook over medium-high heat to soften shallots. Lower heat and reduce liquid by 75 percent; stir in cream and reduce by ½. Slowly whisk in butter over gentle heat. Remove from heat and add lemon and salt; stir and strain. Keep warm in a warm water bath. Yields about 2 cups.

MILTON INN'S ELEANORA SALAD

1 bunch watercress
2 stalks hearts of palm,
    drained
½ head Belgian endive,
    washed

2 large mushrooms, sliced
½ Granny Smith apple, sliced
House Vinaigrette (recipe
    below)

Wash watercress and trim away all but leafy portion; place in a salad bowl. Add hearts of palm, endive, mushrooms, and apple. Toss to combine. Add House Vinaigrette. Serves 4.

House Vinaigrette

2 egg yolks
2 tablespoons Dijon mustard
1 clove garlic, chopped
2 tablespoons Parmesan
    cheese, grated

2 cups olive oil
5½ ounces red wine vinegar
salt and white pepper to taste

Place first 4 ingredients in a blender or food processor and blend. Slowly add olive oil through the feed tube. As mixture thickens, add vinegar, salt, and pepper. Yields over 2 cups.

The Manor Tavern

Route 138
MONKTON

$\mathcal{J}$ tell you, some women have all the luck. In 1667, Charles Calvert, the third Lord Baltimore, was riding through a lush area of Maryland on his way to smoke the peace pipe with the Indians when he made the sage decision to retain ten thousand acres of "this faire land." In 1713, he made a gift of the land to his fourth bride and specified that it be called "My Lady's Manor."

That lady was indeed lucky to receive this parcel of land, which was once the rich hunting and camping ground of the Piscataway Indians, the southern branch of the powerful Susquehannock tribe. I'm sure she would be pleased today with the lovely restaurant called The Manor Tavern, located on her former property.

Lunch
11:30 A.M. until 3:00 P.M.
Monday through Saturday

Dinner
5:30 P.M. until 10:00 P.M.
Tuesday through Saturday

4:00 P.M. until 9:00 P.M.
Sunday

Sunday Brunch
Noon until 3:00 P.M.

For reservations
(recommended)
call (301) 771-4840

I traveled on Old York Road through a fairyland that was in the process of giving birth to spring. Originally an Indian trail, Old York Road became the main north-south thoroughfare as traffic through the colonies progressed. Many shops, taverns, and stables were built after nearby St. James Church was begun in 1750. The Manor Tavern was a stable during that period, serving both the customers of Slade's Tavern, located directly across the road, and the parishioners of the church.

The restaurant now features American cuisine while paying homage to traditional Maryland fare. The decor is a subtle blend of rustic and upscale in this land of fast horses and clever foxes. In a restaurant that treads so many delicate lines, I chose a California Chardonnay from Fetzer to accompany my appetizers of Pita Crab Dip and Soft-Shell Crab. I followed this with a hearty cup of Bourbon Street Gumbo, made with shellfish, sausage, and Cajun spices. The Manor Tavern offers a number of interesting salads and sandwiches. I sampled the Tuscany Bread Salad, which combines mozzarella, huge croutons, and tomatoes in a delicious Balsamic Vinaigrette.

Even though the day was chilly, the sun came out on the lovely new flagstone patio, so I took my Blackberry Cobbler and coffee outside. During this event, I learned that fine food and revelry aren't the only claims to fame here. Between 1773 and 1781, George Washington patronized Slade's Tavern on his frequent trips between Mount Vernon and Philadelphia. The Manor Tavern doesn't claim that "Washington slept here," but it is proud to have had his horse as one of its first guests.

THE MANOR TAVERN'S TUSCANY BREAD SALAD

3 cups mixed salad greens
5 to 6 Roma tomatoes,
* chopped*
4 ounces mozzarella cheese,
* cubed*

¾ cup herb croutons
Balsamic Vinaigrette (recipe
* below)*

Toss first 4 ingredients in a mixing bowl. Add Balsamic Vinaigrette to taste. Serves 4.

Balsamic Vinaigrette

2 egg yolks
1 cup olive oil
¼ cup balsamic vinegar

1 tablespoon garlic, diced
1 tablespoon sugar
1 teaspoon honey

Whip egg yolks until stiff. Slowly drizzle in oil, beating continuously. Add vinegar and beat until well mixed. Add garlic, sugar, and honey and mix until incorporated. Yields 1½ cups.

Note: Vinaigrette can be prepared in a food processor.

THE MANOR TAVERN'S PITA CRAB DIP

8 ounces cream cheese,
  softened
1 tablespoon Old Bay seasoning
8 ounces crabmeat (lump or
  backfin)

2 heaping tablespoons provolone cheese
pita bread chips
1 to 2 scallions, diced
½ medium tomato, diced

Blend cream cheese with Old Bay seasoning until smooth. Stir in crabmeat, being careful not to break down crabmeat texture. Spoon into bowl and sprinkle provolone over top. Garnish with pita chips, scallions, and tomato. Serves 4 to 6.

THE MANOR TAVERN'S FRUIT COBBLER

1 stick butter or margarine
2½ cups all-purpose flour
2½ cups sugar
4 cups fresh fruit (peaches,
  blueberries, or blackberries)

1 tablespoon lemon juice
2 teaspoons baking powder
2 cups milk
1 cup nuts (optional)

Melt butter in a 9- by 13- by 2-inch baking pan. In a medium mixing bowl, combine ½ cup flour with ½ cup sugar and toss with fresh fruit and lemon juice. In a separate bowl, mix remaining flour, baking powder, remaining sugar, and milk. Place fruit mixture in pan and sprinkle nuts evenly over top, if desired. Pour pastry dough over fruit mixture. Cook in a preheated 350-degree oven for about 40 minutes or until firm.

Cockey's Tavern

216 East Main Street
WESTMINSTER

$\mathcal{W}$ ould the South have won more battles if the illustrious J. E. B. Stuart and his Confederate troops had pursued Union soldiers rather than the maids at Cockey's Tavern? The legend is that the troops enjoyed more than room and board when they stayed at the tavern during a skirmish with Union forces in the neighborhood in 1863.

Twenty-five years earlier, the tavern had been Dr. William Willis's handsome brick residence and the meeting place for the first session of circuit court in the newly formed Carroll County. Other guests at Cockey's Tavern were travelers on the Baltimore-Pittsburgh Stagecoach and poker players whose stakes were sometimes whole herds of cattle that changed hands overnight.

Those gamblers, of course, wouldn't recognize the place today, although the lounge has original dentil work, raised paneling, and one of the house's prized bay windows. The walls are covered with portraits of nineteenth-century families and famous people. These paintings take a mysterious tumble now and then, suggesting the presence of a ghost. It would be easy to pick a target, since diners usually claim the same seats each time they visit. One day, General Grant's picture fell on a lawyer who regularly lunches in the room next to the lounge.

Having heard that story, Gordon and I sat at a table where we could keep an eye on General Grant in the dining room and General Stuart at the bar (a converted church pew). It seemed appropriate in a high-stakes place to order Clams Casino, cooked in butter with spring onions—an ingredient often specified in recipes at Cockey's Tavern.

The chef describes the restaurant's cuisine as American but says his background is classical French. Having apprenticed under a chef who served both General de Gaulle and Jacqueline Kennedy, he now teaches a gourmet cooking class.

Meals

11:00 A.M. until 10:00 P.M.
Monday through Friday

3:00 P.M. until 11:00 P.M.
Saturday

Noon until 8:00 P.M.
Sunday

For reservations
(recommended)
call (410) 848-3664
or (410) 848-4202

I picked up a wonderful lesson on making pie dough. I was eager to get home and try the technique—putting the flour and frozen margarine into a food processor and taking out smooth dough, half of which (the upper crust) is then rolled in sugar. I'm delighted to say it worked. Fruit pies made this way at Cockey's are Blueberry, Peach, and Apple. I used peaches, cut in halves as the chef suggested.

Of the Veal Normande, the chef says, "Let the veal speak for itself." And who needs to say more about veal scaloppine with mushrooms, cream, and white wine—provided there's a little spring onion?

COCKEY'S TAVERN'S PEACH PIE

Crust

3 cups all-purpose flour
1 cup frozen margarine

⅓ cup very cold water
flour and sugar for rolling dough

Put flour in a food processor. Leave it on highest speed and add small pieces of margarine a few at a time. Allow 30 seconds for margarine to break up, then add water in a slow, steady stream. Dough will bind itself together and form a ball. Divide dough into 2 parts. Roll bottom crust on a floured surface and fit it into a 9-inch pie pan. Roll both sides of remaining dough on a surface sprinkled with sugar and set aside to use as upper crust.

Filling

8 fresh peaches
⅔ cup sugar

1 teaspoon or more cinnamon
3 tablespoons cornstarch

Skin peaches, cut in half, and remove pits. Combine sugar, cinnamon, and cornstarch. Toss peach halves in this mixture to coat thoroughly. Place coated halves in pie shell along with remaining sugar-cinnamon mixture. Fit sugared upper crust over filling. Bake in a 350-degree oven for 1 hour or until sugar browns on top. Do not overcook fruit. Yields 1 covered 9-inch pie.

COCKEY'S TAVERN'S VEAL NORMANDE

4 tablespoons butter
1 pound veal scaloppine
flour for dusting
12 mushrooms, sliced thin

4 spring onions, sliced thin
8 ounces white wine
8 ounces heavy cream

Melt butter in a heavy skillet, heating until very hot. Dust veal lightly with flour and sauté in hot butter for 1 minute on each side. Remove veal to a warm platter. Add mushrooms, spring onions, and wine to pan, raise heat, and boil about 1 minute. Add cream and boil again, stirring, for 1 minute or until sauce thickens. Pour sauce over veal and serve immediately. Serves 4.

COCKEY'S TAVERN'S CLAMS CASINO

Casino Butter

½ pound softened butter
3 spring onions, chopped
½ medium green pepper,
  chopped fine

4 ounces pimento, chopped
juice of half a lemon
1 clove garlic

Combine all ingredients and mix well.

6 strips bacon

24 clams on the half shell

Cut each bacon strip crosswise into 4 pieces. Place 1 rounded teaspoon of Casino Butter over each clam and cover with 1 piece of bacon. Bake in a 450- to 475-degree oven for 5 to 7 minutes, or broil 4 to 5 minutes, until bacon is crisp. Yields 4 to 6 appetizer servings.

Maggie's

Washington Road at Green Street
WESTMINSTER

ounding a bend in the road one night, Gordon and I discovered Maggie's. The date *1903* caught my eye, so we stopped to go into the barroom, originally operated by Maggie and Levi Zahn. Before their time, the building was a store selling tools and farm implements, with the owner backpacking through the valleys around Westminster to reach his customers.

During the Zahns' lifetime, Maggie ran the bar and Levi ran a blacksmith shop in the back of the building. For several decades except during Prohibition, Maggie's continued to sell drinks. Later, as the Green Street Inn, it reportedly served the best steamed crabs ever eaten. After other owners and vacancies, the building was bought and reopened in 1976 as Maggie's. The name was restored because the owner had childhood recollections of Maggie, whom he remembered as a woman who always wore a black apron. When Maggie's remodeled the former blacksmith shop into a dining room, the hearth and fireplace were styled to look like the type Levi might have used.

Maggie's prides itself on casual charm and a menu that's both Continental and traditional Maryland. I ordered a dish listed on the menu as one of "Maggie's Favorites"—Chicken Livers with Mushrooms and Tomatoes. The waitress said, "That's *everybody's* favorite." Gordon chose Chicken Champagne—strips of chicken fillet and julienned carrots with sliced mushrooms in a champagne gravy. The recipe for Brussels Sprouts Dijonnaise gave me a new way to fix an old-favorite vegetable in a sauce of mustard and cream.

A comfortable room with off-white walls, a brick floor, and exposed wood is called the Ivan Gamber Room because of a nameplate that hangs there. The wooden sign was found in the attic, but no one knew who Ivan Gamber was until a ninety-year-old man walked in

Lunch
11:30 A.M. until 5:00 P.M.
Monday through Saturday

Noon until 10:00 P.M.
Sunday

Dinner
5:00 P.M. until 11:00 P.M.
Monday through Saturday

Noon until 10:00 P.M.
Sunday

For reservations
(recommended)
call (410) 848-1441
or (410) 876-6868

one day. It was probably curiosity that brought him to the place where he had once worked for Levi as a blacksmith, until automobiles became popular and he switched to repairing cars. Ivan liked Maggie's—and the sign with his name on it—so much that he stayed for lunch!

MAGGIE'S BRUSSELS SPROUTS DIJONNAISE

1 pint fresh Brussels sprouts
1½ tablespoons butter
¼ cup chicken stock
¾ cup whipping cream

1½ to 2 tablespoons Dijon
  mustard
salt and pepper to taste
bacon bits
parsley

Wash and trim Brussels sprouts, cut an X in bottoms with a paring knife, and blanch in lightly salted water until tender. Drain. In a skillet, melt butter over medium heat. Add Brussels sprouts and cook until warmed through. Increase heat to high, add chicken stock, and reduce by ½. Stir in cream and mustard. Bring to a rapid boil and reduce until sauce coats a wooden spoon. Add salt and pepper. Brussels sprouts may be topped with crisp bacon bits and chopped parsley. Serves 4.

MAGGIE'S CHICKEN CHAMPAGNE

1½ pounds boneless chicken
  breasts
⅓ cup flour for dredging
⅓ cup oil
4 tablespoons butter
4 medium carrots, peeled,
  julienned, and blanched

½ pound mushrooms, sliced
8 shallots, sliced
1 cup champagne
½ cup dry sherry
1½ cups whipping cream
salt and pepper to taste
fresh parsley

Cut chicken (trimmed of any fat) into strips approximately 1½ by 3 inches and dust lightly with flour. Heat oil in skillet, then add chicken and sauté approximately 2 minutes on each side; remove to a warm platter. Drain oil from skillet and add butter.

Sauté carrots, mushrooms, and shallots until tender. Turn heat to high and add champagne and sherry. Boil until reduced by ½. Add cream and stir to blend. Lower heat and cook until sauce lightly coats a wooden spoon. Add salt and pepper. Pour sauce over chicken. Garnish with sprigs of fresh parsley. Serves 6.

Note: Look in gourmet stores for champagne in 8-ounce bottles, the right amount for this recipe.

MAGGIE'S CHICKEN LIVERS WITH MUSHROOMS AND TOMATOES

oil to coat skillet
1½ pounds fresh chicken livers
½ cup flour for dredging
6 shallots, diced (or 1 small red onion)
½ pound fresh mushrooms, sliced

14-ounce can plum tomatoes
2 cloves garlic, minced
¼ cup dry sherry
2 cups Jus Lie *(recipe below)*
salt and pepper to taste
cooked rice for 6

Heat oil in a heavy skillet. Dredge chicken livers lightly in flour and sauté approximately 5 minutes until brown and slightly crisp. Remove from skillet to a warm, covered platter. Drain oil from pan and add shallots, mushrooms, tomatoes, and garlic. Cook until mushrooms become tender. Turn heat to high, add sherry, and ignite. Bring to a rapid boil and add *Jus Lie* and livers. Simmer for approximately 5 minutes over medium heat. Add salt and pepper and serve over rice. Serves 4 to 6.

Jus Lie

4 tablespoons butter
4 tablespoons flour

12 ounces canned beef broth

Melt butter in a skillet. Add flour and stir until there is a smooth roux. Add beef broth a little at a time, stirring to keep sauce smooth.

Antrim 1844

30 Trevanion Road
TANEYTOWN

$\mathcal{W}$ould General George Meade, who watched his Union troops' movements at the 1863 Battle of Gettysburg from Antrim's widow's walk, ever have believed that this mansion would someday become a connoisseur's dream of fantasy dining? Probably not. The change occurred when the Federal-style mansion with Greek and Italianate over-tones was rescued by Dorothy and Richard Mollett in the 1990s.

A five-course prix fixe dinner is served daily.

Cocktails begin at 6:30 P.M.

Dinner is served at 7:30 P.M.

For reservations (required) call (800) 858-1844 or (410) 756-6812

Built in 1844 by Colonel Andrew Ege as a wedding gift to his daughter, the estate was named for Ege's home in Antrim, Ireland. The Molletts have transformed the brick mansion into an elegant inn and restaurant, maintaining its tasteful affluence with a combination of antique furnishings and today's luxuries. Manager Steven Dearie borrowed from French dining service to complement chef Sharon Ashburn's inspired American cuisine, which utilizes French techniques.

My prix fixe dining experience (with choices) began in the pub with crabmeat hors d'oeuvres and moved to the living room, where a musician was playing a Knabe piano.

The scent of fresh flowers was throughout the mansion, as well as throughout the Smokehouse Dining Room in an outbuilding, the Outdoor Cafe in the old root cellar, the veranda, and the house's formal dining room. A bouquet of lilacs graced my table's linen cloth, set with sterling silver and Antrim's own handsome, gold-rimmed white china and crystal, which glowed in the flickering firelight from the black marble fireplace. I sampled the Cream of Asparagus with Red Pepper Bisque. My appetizer, Herb-Marinated Scallops with Polenta and Eggplant Ratatouille, neatly combined three distinctly different recipe persuasions on the same plate.

I was served a crisp Salad, followed by an intermezzo of refreshing Raspberry and Strawberry Sorbet to cleanse the palate. I chose the Roasted Pheasant with Cranberry Pan Gravy, which proved a tart way to discover the robust pleasures of this game delicacy. With the entrée, this superb restaurant offered Herbed Mashed Potatoes, a steamed Cabbage and Carrots combination, and young Green Beans prepared al dente.

The desserts that evening were a seductively rich Chocolate Pâté and a smooth and creamy homemade Coconut Ice Cream.

Overnight guests at Antrim are treated as if it's their last day on earth, from the appetizer course to the bubble-bath Jacuzzi before a roaring fireplace that's been set with champagne and strawberries dipped in chocolate. Soft classical music plays in the background, a fragrant rose lies on your pillow beside a chocolate, and a decanter of port awaits you at your bedside table. And the wooden butler "James" stands outside your door for your breakfast coffee, juice, muffins, and newspaper as you snuggle onto a goose-down mattress in a lace-canopied bed.

ANTRIM 1844'S ROASTED PHEASANT WITH CRANBERRY PAN GRAVY

2 2-pound pheasants
salt and pepper
1 small onion, quartered
juice of half a lemon
2 large sprigs of thyme or 1
    teaspoon dried thyme
1 tablespoon vegetable oil
½ cup sweet cranberry juice

2 cups pheasant stock or
    chicken stock
1 cup fresh cranberries
salt and freshly ground
    pepper to taste
1 to 2 tablespoons sugar
    (optional)

Clean birds with cold water; dry with paper towels. Salt and pepper birds inside and out. Combine onion, lemon juice, and thyme and stuff into pheasants. Truss birds securely. Heat oil in a skillet on medium-high and sear birds on all sides. Remove birds to a pan and place in a preheated 400-degree oven for 35 to 50 minutes or until a meat thermometer placed in birds' thigh registers 160 degrees. Pour off excess fat and deglaze pan with cranberry juice. Reduce volume to 2 tablespoons. Add stock to pan and reduce by half or until slightly thickened. Add cranberries and simmer until cranberries pop. Add salt and pepper. If gravy is too tart, add sugar a tablespoon at a time. When birds are done, remove meat from bones. Place on warm plates and ladle cranberry gravy over top. Serves 2.

ANTRIM 1844'S HERBED MASHED POTATOES

2 pounds Yukon potatoes, well
   scrubbed
2 tablespoons kosher salt
¼ cup diced garlic

¼ cup fresh herbs, chopped
¼ cup butter
¼ cup heavy cream
salt and pepper to taste

Cover potatoes with cold water and salt. Bring to a boil and simmer until tender. Drain. When potatoes are slightly cooled but still hot, peel and place in a bowl with garlic, herbs, and butter. Mash to desired consistency. Stir in cream and season with salt and pepper. Serves 4.

ANTRIM 1844'S CHOCOLATE PÂTÉ

1¼ cups heavy cream
¼ cup butter
1 pound semisweet chocolate,
   chopped into ½-inch pieces
1 cup toasted almonds, ground

1 cup assorted whole nuts,
   toasted and ground
zest of half an orange
1 ounce Grand Marnier
1 cup assorted dried fruits,
   diced or ground

Bring cream and butter to a boil. Remove from heat and stir in chocolate until melted. Stir in remaining ingredients. Line a loaf pan with plastic wrap and pour in chocolate mixture. Cover and refrigerate overnight. Slice into ¼-inch pieces. Arrange 2 to 3 pieces per dish. Yields about 96 pieces.

Cozy Restaurant

105 Frederick Road
THURMONT

_E_ veryone has a different idea of Shangri-la, and a person's dream will even vary depending on his needs. But the evening that I crossed the tiny bridge opposite the Cozy Country Inn's waterwheel and stepped into a bedroom suite where a crackling fire cut the evening's chill, I responded to the wind-down message. The rustic atmosphere of this establishment, nestled in the lap of the Catoctin Mountains, was what I needed.

Apparently, it was also what was needed by the Russian entourage that accompanied Leonid Brezhnev to Camp David in 1979. The Cozy is located just eight miles from Camp David, and Russian security came to check out the establishment.

Mid-April through first week in January

Meals

11:00 A.M. until 8:45 P.M.
Monday through Thursday

11:00 A.M. until 8:30 P.M.
Friday

8:00 A.M. until 9:15 P.M.
Saturday

8:00 A.M. until 8:45 P.M.
Sunday

Continental breakfast is served to inn guests beginning at 7:00 A.M.

To check on winter hours or to make reservations call (301) 271-7373

Owners Mary Freeze and her son Jerry tried to persuade the Russians to seek more luxurious accommodations, but it was too late—they had already tasted the Cozy's juicy Steaks and northern Maryland country cooking. A direct telephone line to Moscow was installed. For over ten days, the Russians made heavy use of the Country Room's "Groaning Board," which is laden with eighty items, not counting the assortment of thirty homemade desserts.

Like the Russians, Rebecca enjoys the Cozy's Steaks and has gone out of her way to revisit the restaurant through the years for this great entrée. On each visit, she takes a nibble of the Hot Apple Fritters and the variety of home-baked White, Cinnamon, and Raisin Breads, and more than a nibble of the legendary Turkey Corn Soup.

The Cozy's wine cellar contains many popular imported and domestic vintages. You'll be certain to find something good to go with the delicious Roast Turkey, Country Fried Chicken, and mildly cured Ham, which is neither too sweet nor too salty.

Everyone can tell that desserts are my downfall. The Cozy's array of prizewinning desserts—some of them from the bake-offs the restaurant held in previous years—are enticingly displayed. We sampled the Chocolate Eclair Pie and my all-time favorite—Mexican Wedding Cake. Try this one for your next party.

We took a tour and were surprised by the Cozy's great size. In her sixty-plus years at the Cozy, Mary Freeze has seen it grow from twelve stools to a seating of almost 750. On the bulletin board, the collection of photos of film, press, sports, and political celebrities who have discovered the Cozy continues to grow.

COZY RESTAURANT'S MEXICAN WEDDING CAKE

2 cups cake flour
2 cups sugar
2 teaspoons baking soda
¼ teaspoon salt
2 medium eggs
2½ cups pineapple, crushed
2 teaspoons vanilla

1 cup pecans, chopped
Cream Cheese Frosting
   (recipe below)
3 or 4 whole pineapple slices
   for garnish
cherries for garnish

Mix together flour, sugar, baking soda, and salt. Add eggs and crushed pineapple and mix until well combined. Add vanilla and mix about 30 seconds. Fold in pecans. Pour into a greased 9- by 12- by 2-inch pan and bake for 30 to 35 minutes in a preheated 325-degree oven, or pour into a Bundt cake pan and bake for about 60 minutes. Test with cake ⌐ster for doneness. Frost cake with Cream Cheese Frosting and garnish with pineapple slices and cherries. Yields 1 cake.

Cream Cheese Frosting

8 ounces cream cheese,
   softened
1 stick margarine or butter,
   softened

2 cups powdered sugar, sifted
1 teaspoon vanilla

Combine cream cheese and margarine in an electric mixer. Add sugar and mix until incorporated. Yields frosting for 1 cake.

COZY RESTAURANT'S TURKEY CORN SOUP

7 cups turkey broth, homemade or commercial
1 cup celery, chopped
1-pound can whole-kernel
  corn
2 tablespoons butter
¼ teaspoon pepper
1 tablespoon plus 2 teaspoons
  sugar
¼ teaspoon thyme

½ tablespoon parsley
½ tablespoon chicken bouillon
½ tablespoon Accent or
  monosodium glutamate
  (optional)
1 to 2 drops yellow food
  coloring (optional)
6 tablespoons flour
1 egg yolk

In a large soup pot, combine turkey broth and all ingredients except flour and egg yolk. Cook for 45 minutes, stirring often. Mix flour with egg yolk and crumble on top of soup. Stir and cook for 10 minutes more. Serves 6.

Mealey's

8 Main Street
NEW MARKET

$\mathcal{J}$ohn Robert's 1793 log-cabin store is retained within the brick walls of a three-story Federal-style building on Main Street. The building later functioned as the Utz Hotel and still remains in step with New Market's spirit of preservation as the antique capital of the world. Today, a restaurant named Mealey's is proud to occupy a building that has served many of New Market's needs.

In 1905, several of the Utz Hotel's upstairs bedrooms were converted into offices for the C & P Telephone Company. An Utz grand-daughter remembers the oft-repeated tale her mother told of her employment at the telephone company. At age nine, when not in school, she worked as a relief operator and occasionally had to be hidden when telephone company supervisors suddenly materialized for on-site inspections.

The building has housed many occupants, including high-school students when the new high school was under construction. After the building became Mealey's, Dick Mealey invited Washington dignitaries to dine at the restaurant. Mrs. Mealey, who wanted to impress her guests, served Dick's homemade wine. She especially impressed one guest who was an Internal Revenue Service employee. Unfortunately, those were Prohibition days, and in no time, wine disappeared from the premises.

Today, owners Jose and Pat Salaverri offer over seventy wines, including regional, domestic, and international vintages. I chose a crisp white regional Elk Run to go with my appetizer, Jumbo Shrimp Cocktail, and my Maryland Crab Cake, made with the backfin crabmeat that I never seem to tire of when I'm in Maryland. Mealey's cuisine, a contemporized colonial American, more than deserves the name of "comfort food."

I wanted to experience more of the flavor of this restaurant, with

---

Lunch
11:30 A.M. until 2:30 P.M.
Friday and Saturday

Dinner
5:00 P.M. until 9:00 P.M.
Tuesday through Friday

4:30 P.M. until 9:00 P.M.
Saturday

Noon until 8:00 P.M.
Sunday

For reservations
call (301) 865-5488

its exposed brick walls and tasteful decor, so I moved into the Pump Room for a dessert of delicious Pecan Pie. The old water pump standing in the rear of the room was originally the hotel's only water supply. In those early days, the building was also a rest stop for thirsty travelers and their horses. This pump served them, as well as all the hotel's guests.

On my return visit to Mealey's, I was happy to see that the old Wurlitzer jukebox still rings out old tunes for the price of a nickel.

MEALEY'S PECAN PIE

4 eggs
1 cup sugar
1 cup dark corn syrup
1 tablespoon flour
½ teaspoon salt

4 tablespoons melted butter
2 teaspoons vanilla
1 cup pecans
1 unbaked 9-inch pie shell

Beat eggs by hand. Add sugar and whip together with electric mixer. Add syrup and mix until combined. Add flour and salt, whipping until combined, and blend in melted butter. Add vanilla and mix until incorporated. Fold in pecans and pour into pie shell. Bake in a 350-degree oven for 50 minutes or until knife inserted in center comes out clean. Yields 1 pie.

MEALEY'S OLD-FASHIONED CLUB SANDWICH

Sauce

2 tablespoons butter
2 tablespoons plain flour
1 cup milk

10-ounce can mushroom soup
½ cup cheddar cheese, grated

Melt butter in a skillet over medium-high heat. Add flour and stir until a paste forms. Add milk and stir until combined. Add mushroom soup and stir until blended. Add cheese and stir until melted.

8 *slices white bread*　　　　　8 *slices tomato*
8 *thin slices ham*　　　　　　8 *slices bacon, fried*
8 *thin slices turkey*

Lay the bread in a large, flat pan and cover each slice with equal portions of ham, turkey, and tomato. Ladle sauce over all and heat in a 375-degree oven for 5 minutes. Serve 2 open-faced sandwiches on each plate, topped with bacon. Serves 4.

MEALEY'S COLESLAW

1 *small cabbage*　　　　　　1 *tablespoon cider vinegar*
½ *cup mayonnaise*　　　　　½ *teaspoon salt*
1 *tablespoon sugar*　　　　　½ *teaspoon pepper*
¼ *cup evaporated milk*

Shred cabbage. Add remaining ingredients and season to taste. Cover and refrigerate. Serves 4 to 6.

Bushwaller's

209 North Market Street
FREDERICK

*F*rederick is a town that honors its historical past without losing pace with the future. You are firmly anchored in both periods when you dine at Bushwaller's. Familiar dishes are served in innovative ways, such as the sandwiches that are garnished with fresh vegetables rather than the traditional chips or fries.

Lunch
11:30 A.M. until 4:00 P.M.
Daily

For reservations
(recommended)
call (301) 694-5697

A real historic favorite is the Jubal Early Bird. This sandwich is named after General Jubal Early, the Confederate who threatened to burn Frederick unless his ransom was met. So the city fathers gathered bushel baskets of money and left them on the steps of city hall. As a transplanted Westerner who grew up in the South, I find it funny that Southern history books depict only the Yankees using those tactics. Hmm.

One of the charms of Frederick is that it has kept its early Federal-style village atmosphere. Bushwaller's, which recaptures the feeling of a neighborhood tavern, was built as a private home in 1840. Sometime around the turn of the century, the home became Steiner's Drug Store. It later became a dry-goods store dealing in contraband cigarettes, and when the Bushwaller brothers found it in 1980, it had become a liquor store.

Because I love the combination of fried oysters, ham, and tomatoes, I found that the Bay and Barnyard Sandwich could fill a hungry cavity to overflowing. I sampled the Sautéed Chicken Breast and learned that it was as attractive to look at as it was to taste. Or you might want to order the tasty Shrimp, Lobster, and Crab Sauté, which nutrition experts say adds to your brain power. Or try reproducing it at home, as this is a great and quick recipe to make.

Dieters may be lucky enough to order Alligator Tail, which tastes like veal, is very short on calories, and is served when obtainable. Or you can lunch on a Greenleaf and Almond Salad or the California Pita to keep your jeans from pinching. However, it won't help if, like me, you take in Bushwaller's famous Mud Pie or wonderful Strawberry Pie when strawberries are in season.

Anyone who finds himself near Frederick on St. Patrick's Day should join in what they call the "Pub Crawl." All true or adopted Irish gather not to charm the snakes, as St. Paddy did on the celebrated day, but to travel together in the most outlandish costumes that can be assembled. Walking from restaurant to restaurant demands lots of energy, and the throng insists that certain libations are necessary for the pilgrimage.

BUSHWALLER'S SAUTÉED CHICKEN BREAST

4 boneless chicken breasts
flour for dredging
salt and pepper to taste
3 tablespoons butter
12 fresh mushrooms
4 pimentos, sliced fine
4 sprigs parsley, chopped fine

heavy pinch of garlic powder
dash of salt
dash of pepper
¼ cup white wine
wild rice, cooked according to
    package directions

Pound chicken breasts lightly with a meat mallet and dredge in flour seasoned with salt and pepper. Melt butter in a skillet over high heat and sauté chicken on both sides until cooked. Remove chicken and keep warm. Add mushrooms, pimentos, parsley, garlic, salt, and pepper and sauté until tender, adding more butter if needed. Stir in wine and cook for 4 to 5 minutes. Serve chicken with wild rice. Ladle sauce over chicken. Serves 4.

BUSHWALLER'S BAY AND BARNYARD SANDWICH

1 ounce seafood cocktail sauce
1 tablespoon mayonnaise
1 to 2 dashes Tabasco sauce
salt and pepper to taste
3 slices wheat bread (or your
    choice of bread, but not
    hoagy type)
2 slices honey-baked ham

1 to 2 tablespoons light
    vegetable oil
3 breaded Chesapeake Bay
    oysters
2 leaves lettuce
2 slices tomato
1 slice Swiss cheese

Mix cocktail sauce with mayonnaise, Tabasco sauce, salt, and pepper. Toast bread. Spread each slice of bread with mayonnaise mixture and set aside. Heat ham in a 425-degree oven until hot. Pour oil in a skillet set on medium-high and pan-fry oysters until done; drain. To assemble, layer one bread slice with lettuce, tomato, hot ham, and cheese. Top with second slice of bread and layer with lettuce, tomato, and oysters. Top with third slice of bread and cut in club-sandwich style. Yields 1 sandwich.

BUSHWALLER'S SHRIMP, LOBSTER, AND CRAB SAUTÉ

12 ounces medium shrimp, peeled and cleaned
½ cup seasoned flour
4 tablespoons butter
1¼ cups fresh mushrooms, sliced
½ cup scallions, sliced
5 tablespoons fresh garlic, chopped

4 sprigs parsley, chopped fine
6 ounces fresh lobster meat
6 ounces lump crabmeat
½ cup sherry
salt and pepper to taste
white rice for 4, cooked according to package directions

Lightly dredge shrimp in flour and shake off excess. Melt the butter in a large skillet over low heat. Sauté shrimp until about done. Stir in mushrooms, scallions, garlic, and parsley and let cook 1 minute. Add lobster, crabmeat, and sherry. Simmer 3 to 4 minutes or until sauce thickens slightly. Season with salt and pepper and serve over hot white rice. Serves 4.

The Province

129 North Market Street
FREDERICK

$\mathcal{N}$o hats were on sale when I ate lunch in the former Mrs. Snyder's Hat Shop, but several women from Frederick told me they remembered when their mothers shopped here for their Sunday best. Those were the days of Mr. John's Originals, when local milliners fashioned ribbons and lace into imaginative designs. Then, alas, hats went out of style.

The property on North Market was first deeded to blacksmith Cudlip Miller, who passed it on to his son with the stipulation that rooms be added to the one-room home. The hat shop occupied the building some years back, but today a restaurant incorporates the original house and its additions. The restaurant is called The Province, Circa 1767. The word *province* refers to Maryland's having been a province, rather than a state, before the Revolutionary War.

Lunch
11:30 A.M. until 3:00 P.M.
Monday through Friday

Dinner
5:30 P.M. until 9:00 P.M.
Tuesday through Thursday

5:30 P.M. until 10:00 P.M.
Friday and Saturday

4:00 P.M. until 8:00 P.M.
Sunday

Saturday Brunch
11:30 A.M. until 3:00 P.M.

Sunday Brunch
11:00 A.M. until 2:30 P.M.

For reservations
(requested)
call (301) 663-1441

On my tour of The Province, I was taken through the former hat shop into the original room, whose brick walls are partly covered with quilts that serve as both baffle and decoration. One prized quilt contains the names of all those employed at The Province at the time the quilt was sewn by the mother of the chef. Beyond that room is a garden room with a brick floor. On the patio, tea was brewing in the sun beside an herb garden.

After the tour, I sat in the front room with a glass of Chablis to wait for lunch. While welcoming her guests by name, manager Nancy Floria explained that she and her husband had wanted to have a really good place to eat without going into Washington. The Province was established at a time when Frederick lacked such places. Now, the surge of growth in the town would make Cudlip Miller proud.

The Province is best known for its desserts. Whole cakes are available with notice to the chef. I was intrigued to hear about a wedding cake made from seven different kinds of cheesecake.

A prettier dessert tray I've never seen: Queen Mother Chocolate Almond Cake, Kahlúa Pecan Pie, Cheesecake with Lemon Glaze. I ate the recommended Mocha Nut Torte and was pleased with the creamy, crumbly choice. It was a perfect finish to my meal of Parisian Poulet, a combination of chicken, mushrooms, and Brie that is the most popular entrée at The Province. I later served it and the torte when Dawn O'Brien and two other collaborators on this cookbook series came to my house for lunch. We ate and ate, then happily smiled for publicity pictures.

THE PROVINCE'S MOCHA NUT TORTE

Torte

6 eggs, separated
1 cup sugar
½ cup vanilla wafers, ground

¼ cup flour
1 cup walnuts, ground fine

Beat egg yolks until light, then add ¾ cup sugar, mixing until thick and pale. Beat egg whites, gradually adding ¼ cup sugar, until stiff. Sift together vanilla wafers and flour and add walnuts. Add the nut-wafer mixture alternately with the egg white mixture into the egg yolk mixture. Turn into two 9-inch cake pans lined with unbuttered parchment paper. Bake in a 350-degree oven for 20 minutes or until cake tester comes out clean. Remove from pans and cool on rack.

Icing

½ cup sugar
2 tablespoons cornstarch
1 cup strong coffee, cold
1 ounce semisweet chocolate,
   melted

1 tablespoon butter
1 teaspoon vanilla
1 cup heavy cream
chocolate shavings for
   garnish

Mix sugar and cornstarch in a saucepan. Gradually add coffee and chocolate. Bring to a boil and cook for 1 minute. Add butter and vanilla, then set aside to cool. When cake is ready to frost, whip cream until thick and fold into cooled mocha mixture. Spread frosting on 1 layer, place other layer on top, and spread remaining frosting. Sprinkle chocolate shavings over top. Refrigerate at least 1 hour before serving. Serves 10 to 12.

THE PROVINCE'S PARISIAN POULET

4 ounces clarified butter
2 whole chicken breasts
flour for dredging
1 egg, well beaten
1 cup sliced mushrooms

salt and pepper to taste
4 ounces ripened Brie
2 to 3 ounces amontillado
sherry
cooked rice or couscous

In a large skillet, heat clarified butter until it is hot but not smoking. Dip chicken in flour, then in egg. Place chicken pieces in skillet 1 at a time, shaking skillet vigorously to prevent sticking. Brown on both sides. Remove chicken and set aside. Add mushrooms to skillet, lightly salt and pepper, and sauté about 1 minute. Replace chicken in skillet and top each piece with a slice of Brie. Add sherry and ignite. Remove pan from heat. Cover pan for a moment to melt the cheese. Place chicken on beds of rice or couscous and pour mushroom mixture over chicken. Serves 2 or more.

Stone Manor Country Club

5820 Carroll Boyer Road
MIDDLETOWN

$\mathcal{F}$rom Stone Manor's upscale, rustic Stone Dining
Room, you can see South Mountain, a site that witnessed one of
the Civil War's most strategic
battles. It's hard to imagine that
this rural valley that runs beside
Catoctin Creek was once alive
with the thunder of cannon fire,
because now you have to listen
for sounds. They come when
wind ruffles the trees and birds
chatter or when classical music
plays throughout the manor's gra-
ciously appointed dining rooms.

Lunch
11:00 A.M. until 2:00 P.M.
Tuesday through Saturday

Dinner
6:00 P.M. until 9:00 P.M.
Tuesday through Saturday

4:00 P.M. until 6:00 P.M.
Sunday

For reservations
(required)
call (301) 473-5454

William Rice is believed to have built the initial four-room stone
farm home in the 1700s. In 1802, Rice's son James sold it to brothers Joseph and Benjamin Penn for 637 pounds and 10 shillings. The
Penn brothers added four rooms with exterior walls made of stone
quarried from Catoctin Creek and secured the stone structure with
the same iron plowshares that can still be seen near the fireplace in
the Stone Dining Room. Through the years, succeeding owners have
added an additional nine rooms. The manor's newest addition came
in the 1970s, when the estate was named "Two Sons Farm," perhaps
in honor of William Rice, who had two sons.

I sat beside the old fireplace in a handsome burgundy tufted chair
and wished that I had a week rather than just a night and day to
spend here. The manor's gentle ambiance is like that of an English
country estate. The views of the Catoctin Mountains are superb.

Before my appetizer of Black Ham, Whole-Grain Mustard,
Raspberry Glace, and Rye Toast arrived, I couldn't imagine the food
combination. But I soon learned that chef John Walla is astute at
blending unusual ingredients. The secret that makes the dish work is
the Raspberry Glace. Roasted Tomato Soup with lump crabmeat,
grilled brioche croutons, and avocado became a delicious fusion of
unlikely ingredients. A demi-entrée of Smoked Salmon and Potatoes
was another tantalizer, served with a French rosé.

To cleanse the palate, a tiny scoop of Mango Sorbet with Kiwi

Coulis was offered. Then it was on to the entrée. Although the meal is a five-course prix fixe offering, guests do have a choice of courses. I opted for the Ancho Chili Marinated Loin of Pork with Caramelized Red Onions. The chili gave the succulent pork real personality, and I equally enjoyed a vegetable dish called Tian of Zucchini, Yellow Squash, Red Pepper, and Goat Cheese. The texture and creaminess of the cheese made this dish one I wanted to share with my readers.

I was so satisfied at this meal's conclusion that the only dessert I had room for was more of the Mango Sorbet. Then it was time to wind my way upstairs to a beautiful split-level suite that included a Jacuzzi and an old-fashioned bed that required steps to climb into it. You could say that there's nothing to do here, but by the time you leave, you may feel as did one guest who said, "I didn't realize how much nothing I had to do."

Stone Manor Country Club is not a country club in the usual sense—it doesn't have golf courses, swimming pools, etc. But it does have the most elegant clubhouse—open to the public—that you'll find in Maryland.

STONE MANOR COUNTRY CLUB'S MANGO SORBET WITH KIWI COULIS

7 ounces sugar	rind and juice of 1 lime
1½ cups water	3 very ripe mangoes
rind and juice of 1 lemon	6 egg whites

To form a simple syrup, combine sugar, water, and rinds in a saucepan over medium-high heat. Bring to a boil and boil for 1 minute. Let syrup cool slightly. Meanwhile, peel mangoes and remove seeds. Pour lemon and lime juice over mangoes and purée in a food processor. Gradually add the syrup and egg whites. Process until well combined. Strain the mixture and pour into a shallow 8- by 8- by 2-inch pan. Cover pan tightly with plastic wrap and 2 layers of heavy aluminum foil and put in freezer. When frozen firm, process in food processor to aerate mixture. Refreeze and serve. Yields ½ gallon.

Kiwi Coulis

6 kiwis   mint leaves (optional)
2 tablespoons powdered sugar

Peel kiwis and process with sugar in a food processor. Strain, leaving seeds in for added texture. Drizzle over sorbet and garnish with mint leaves if desired.

STONE MANOR COUNTRY CLUB'S TIAN OF ZUCCHINI, YELLOW SQUASH, RED PEPPER, AND GOAT CHEESE

2 cups goat cheese, crumbled
4 tablespoons pesto (homemade or commercial)
1 medium zucchini, sliced
   diagonally
1 medium yellow squash,
   sliced diagonally
2 roasted red peppers, peeled,
   seeded, and chopped

2 tablespoons olive oil
4 tablespoons balsamic
   vinegar
salt and pepper to taste
6 tablespoons Parmesan
   cheese, grated
garlic croutons

Mix goat cheese and pesto together and set aside. In a medium-size flat pan (preferably earthenware), layer zucchini and yellow squash alternately across the bottom, using about half of each. Place about half the peppers on top of the squash. Combine olive oil, vinegar, salt, and pepper and sprinkle over top, then spread goat cheese mixture on top. Repeat steps. Sprinkle Parmesan over mixture and bake in a preheated 400-degree oven for about 15 minutes until cheese begins to melt. Serve with garlic croutons. Serves 2.

Old South Mountain Inn

Alternate Route 40
BETWEEN BOONSBORO AND MIDDLETOWN

As Daintry, Rebecca, and I followed the ribbon of mountain road, we played the game of pretending we were travelers on this National Trail in the days of stagecoaches and wagons. The landscape surrounding the Old South Mountain Inn is dotted with few buildings even today, so it was easy to imagine how the sight of the inn must have quickened the heartbeats of eighteenth-century travelers in need of refuge. The 1732 Federal-style stone structure with window boxes full of geraniums was a cheerful and welcome sight for us as well.

We decided the spring sun was warm enough for an al fresco sampling of the local Byrd Vineyard's Chardonnay before lunch. Actually, I think we were a little overeager for the seasonal change, because once inside we were glad to be warmed by the thick, fresh, homemade Tomato Soup. Then, while Rebecca enjoyed her Soft-Shell Maryland Crabs and Daintry tackled the German Wurst Plate, I couldn't stop munching on a Green Salad accompanied by the tangiest Curry Dressing. We took our dessert in the lounge, which has been decorated to look much as you might imagine it looked over two hundred years ago.

During the Civil War, this old building played a part in two notorious events. In 1859, the inn was captured and held overnight as an outpost and gathering place for John Brown's followers in the infamous raid on Harpers Ferry. Three years later, it was the Confederate headquarters of General D. H. Hill during the Battle of South Mountain, which was a preliminary to the Battle of Antietam.

Of course, an establishment like this has its ghost. In 1876, Mrs. Madeline Dahlgren purchased the inn and turned it into a private residence. It can't be proved, but the presence that wanders

Lunch
11:30 A.M. until 2:30 P.M.
Saturday

Dinner
5:00 P.M. until 9:00 P.M.
Tuesday through Friday

4:00 P.M. until 10:00 P.M.
Saturday

Noon until 8:00 P.M.
Sunday

Sunday Brunch
10:30 A.M. until 2:00 P.M.

For reservations
(requested)
call (301) 432-6155

like a wisp of cold air through the upstairs is believed to be her spirit. Until recently, the restaurant's chefs were given an upstairs room for convenience. According to the story, each was awakened so frequently by a knock at the door, which produced nothing more than a cool breeze fleeing past, that they all decided that nearness to one's occupation isn't everything.

OLD SOUTH MOUNTAIN INN'S TOMATO SOUP

1 stick butter
3 cubes chicken bouillon
3 stalks celery, chopped fine
1 small onion, chopped fine
¼ cup flour

4 1-pound cans of tomatoes, chopped, juice reserved
3 to 4 cups tomato juice
5½-ounce can evaporated milk
salt and pepper to taste

Melt butter in a skillet with chicken bouillon, stirring to combine. Add celery and onion and sauté until tender. Stir in the flour to make a roux. Lower heat and cook for 10 minutes. Add chopped tomatoes, juice from their cans, and tomato juice. Stir until well mixed, then stir in evaporated milk. Season with salt and pepper. Serves 10 to 12.

OLD SOUTH MOUNTAIN INN'S SOFT-SHELL CRABS

2 tablespoons clarified butter
2 tablespoons oil (or more as needed)
1 large clove garlic, minced
3 medium shallots, chopped fine
3 tablespoons flour

1 teaspoon salt
1 teaspoon pepper
6 small soft-shell crabs
½ cup Riesling wine
½ cup sliced almonds
3 lemon wedges

Heat butter with oil in a large, heavy skillet over low heat. Sauté garlic and shallots until transparent, stirring constantly. Combine flour, salt, and pepper in a brown paper bag and toss crabs in the bag until coated. Place crabs upside down in skillet and sauté over low heat until lightly browned on 1 side. Add ¼ cup of wine and continue to sauté for 3 minutes. Turn crabs over and add remaining wine. Sprinkle almonds over crabs, cover, and simmer for 8 minutes. Serve with lemon wedges. Serves 3.

OLD SOUTH MOUNTAIN INN'S FROZEN PEANUT BUTTER PIE

½ cup cream cheese, softened
1⅓ cups confectioners' sugar
7½ tablespoons smooth
    peanut butter
½ cup heavy cream

1⅛ cups nondairy whipped
    topping
8-inch graham cracker pie
    shell
¼ cup peanuts, chopped fine

Whip cream cheese at low speed until soft and fluffy. Add sugar and peanut butter and beat at medium speed until smooth. Slowly beat in heavy cream. Fold in whipped topping. Pour into pie shell and sprinkle with chopped nuts. Freeze until firm. Yields 1 pie.

L'Osteria

Turkey-Flight Manor off Route 68
CUMBERLAND

$\mathcal{J}$'ve been told that what makes a party is not the menu, but the men you sit beside. During my visit to L'Osteria, my attention was drawn to a bearded young man who sat at the next table. With him was a little girl proudly swinging a purse. The man explained the menu to the child, mentioned something they ate at home, and ordered a drink for her and wine for himself. When she offered a toast to

Dinner
5:00 P.M. until 10:00 P.M.
Monday through Saturday

Arrangements can be made for special parties on Sunday or luncheons during the week.

For reservations (recommended) call (301) 777-3553

Mommy, it occurred to me that her mother was the chef. What a role model for a five-year-old!

That chef, wearing a white hat almost as tall as she was, had come to our table earlier to suggest that Gordon and I order one entrée that was a regular menu item (Pollo alla Romana) and one that was a daily special not on the menu (Bay Scallops Sienna). We said we'd also like to sample Veal Maria, the dish created in honor of Vincent Price by restaurateur Maria, who with her husband owns the restaurant and has a hand in the cooking.

Maria lets you know with flashing eyes and lilting voice that the cuisine at L'Osteria is authentic northern Italian. She comes from Bologna and loves to cook. She made me feel like a guest in her own home, where, as hostess, she was overseeing a competent chef's preparation of my meal.

As we looked and listened and sipped Chianti, we also tasted the Insalata de Casa. The sight of that oil-and-vinegar-dressed house salad, with radishes and cherry tomatoes perfectly lined up on the smallest of romaine leaves, made me imagine a sign on the kitchen door reading, "Artists at Work." Whatever artistic hands arranged the salad probably also fixed the Veal Maria. The plate was dressed up with bits of carrot-orange and parsley-green and a lemon butterfly. (Those garnishes aren't in the recipe, but you can add your own touch to make it pretty.) The chicken was also colorful, with pepper, onion, and tomatoes, and the Bay Scallops Sienna even had color in its name. All three dishes proved as good to taste as to look at.

L'Osteria is part of a motel with a past. Originally called Turkey-Flight Manor, the building has a strong association with the Civil War. Having housed wounded soldiers on its top floor, the building itself was wounded by a cannonball during a battle at nearby Flock's Mill. Walls in the attic still show scribbled reminders that soldiers were here. One Union soldier drew large sketches of two generals who were captured in Cumberland in 1865 by McNeill's Raiders. I wonder whether Vincent Price critiqued that art when he visited L'Osteria.

L'OSTERIA'S BAY SCALLOPS SIENNA

1 pound fresh bay scallops
½ cup dry white wine
1 cup Marinara Sauce (see note on next page)

½ cup sour cream
salt and pepper to taste
½ pound pasta, cooked

Wash and drain scallops, then poach in wine until white. Add Marinara Sauce. Turn off heat and gently blend in sour cream. Season with salt and pepper and serve over pasta of your choice. Serves 4.

L'OSTERIA'S VEAL MARIA

1 pound veal scallops
flour for dredging
¼ pound butter
¾ cup marinated mushrooms

¾ cup marinated artichoke hearts
salt and pepper to taste
½ pound pasta, cooked

Pound veal scallops as thin as possible and dredge lightly in flour. Sauté veal in butter until meat juices are yellow, *not pink*. Add mushrooms and artichoke hearts and heat through. Season with salt and pepper and serve over pasta of your choice. Serves 4.

olive oil to coat skillet
4 whole chicken breasts,
   deboned and cut into strips
1 large green pepper, sliced
   into strips
1 large onion, sliced into thick
   strips

½ cup white wine
1 cup Marinara Sauce (see
   note)
salt and pepper to taste
½ pound pasta, cooked

Heat olive oil in a large skillet. Add chicken strips and cook until white, turning frequently to prevent sticking. Add green pepper and onion and sauté until tender. Deglaze skillet with white wine. Add Marinara Sauce and heat through. Season with salt and pepper and serve over pasta of your choice. Serves 4.

Note: See index for Marinara Sauce, or use 1 cup of chopped, canned tomatoes and their juice, seasoned with sweet basil and oregano to taste. Heat through to develop flavor.

Oxford House Restaurant

The Inn at Walnut Bottom, 18 Greene Street
CUMBERLAND

$\mathcal{I}$t may be a marriage of convenience between Oxford House Restaurant and The Inn at Walnut Bottom, but true love is in the air. Since Maryland has less restrictive marriage laws than Pennsylvania, couples often cross the state line to get married in Cumberland. And since the courthouse is right across the street, The Inn at Walnut Bottom is a natural place to spend a wedding night and celebrate with dinner at Oxford House Restaurant, which also caters for weddings. One night, as a favor to a young man, the maître d' actually brought out an engagement ring under a dessert-plate cover.

Lunch
11:00 A.M. until 2:30 P.M.
Monday through Saturday

Dinner
5:00 P.M. until 9:30 P.M.
Monday through Saturday

Sunday Brunch
10:00 A.M. until 3:00 P.M.

For reservations
(appreciated)
call (301) 777-7101

The restaurant and the inn are joined in a structure that used to be side-by-side houses, still referred to as the Eliza Cowden House (1820) and the Dent House (1890). The two women who owned them over a hundred years ago would be proud of the women who manage them today: Jaye Miller at Oxford House and Sharon Kazary at Walnut Bottom.

Without any business at the courthouse, Gordon and I had the pleasure of spending a night in The Inn at Walnut Bottom's very attractive Room 2. It was just over the kitchen, but with forty-inch-thick walls, who would know? Leafing through reading material in the adjoining sitting room, we anticipated dinner, which proved to be delightful.

I selected a tartlet of Mushrooms in Creamy Marsala for my appetizer and quickly requested the recipe. I also tasted Gordon's appetizer of velvety Mushroom Soup, and it was as good as it was pretty, with four mushroom slices on top with chives. With glasses of the house Chardonnay, Robert Mondavi Woodbridge, we moved on to our entrées, swapping tastes as we usually do. Picture artichoke bottoms filled with mushrooms, topped by thick rounds of pork fillet, and covered by Béarnaise sauce; that's the prizewinning Fillet of

Pork Grand Hotel, and what a marriage it is. Now picture a strip of salmon dotted with capers, dill, and very thin lemon slices and baked between leaves of romaine lettuce; that dish, Romaine-Wrapped Fillet of Salmon, is a winner in our kitchen.

Diners have their choice of two rooms that contain touches of Sweden—tablecloths and soup tureens—thanks to Jaye Miller's ancestry. The lace-over-blue cloth that covered our table for dinner was changed to a flowered print for breakfast, when we sampled Raisin and Blueberry Muffins, Cinnamon Bread, and Applesauce. Again the food was served with artistry: a cinnamon stick on the plate, an orange slice on top of a half-grapefruit. Is it the influence of the annual Haystack Mountain Art Workshops held here?

George Washington didn't sleep at The Inn at Walnut Bottom, but he was in the neighborhood at several points in his life: first as a surveyor in his teen years, later as General Edward Braddock's assistant during the French and Indian War, and finally as president of the United States during the Whiskey Rebellion. His headquarters cabin is just a short walk down Greene Street, the oldest street in Cumberland, which is on the original National Road. If George Washington could eat at Oxford House Restaurant, what would he order? Maybe Mushrooms in Creamy Marsala.

OXFORD HOUSE RESTAURANT'S MUSHROOMS IN CREAMY MARSALA

2 shallots, chopped fine
2 tablespoons margarine
12 ounces mushrooms (small or quartered)
¾ cup heavy cream

¾ cup sweet Marsala wine
½ cup beef stock or consommé
¼ teaspoon dried tarragon
4 prebaked 4-inch tart shells
parsley

Sauté shallots in margarine. Add mushrooms and sauté 2 minutes more. Add liquids and tarragon. Let simmer and reduce until thick, approximately 10 minutes. Pour hot mixture into tart shells and sprinkle with parsley. Serves 4.

OXFORD HOUSE RESTAURANT'S FILLET OF PORK GRAND HOTEL

12 ounces mushrooms,
    chopped fine
4 tablespoons margarine
1 tablespoon sherry or beef
    stock
salt and pepper to taste

1½-pound pork fillet
flour
12 canned artichoke bottoms
Béarnaise sauce (homemade
    or commercial)

Mushrooms can be prepared ahead and set aside. Simmer mushrooms in 2 tablespoons margarine until all liquid has evaporated. Add sherry or beef stock to enhance flavor. When almost dry, add salt and pepper.

Cut pork into 1-inch-thick pieces, 3 per person. Turn pork in flour seasoned with salt and pepper. Melt 2 tablespoons margarine in skillet and brown pork on both sides, in batches so as not to crowd them in the pan. Then place all pork in the skillet, cover, and simmer on low heat approximately 15 minutes until no longer pink.

Fill artichoke bottoms with mushrooms. Heat briefly in a microwave or a regular oven. Place a piece of fillet on each, 3 to a plate. Pour Béarnaise sauce over fillets and serve. Serves 4.

OXFORD HOUSE RESTAURANT'S ROMAINE-WRAPPED FILLET OF SALMON

4 6-ounce salmon fillets
8 large pieces of romaine
    lettuce
salt and white pepper to taste

1 teaspoon dried dillweed
2 tablespoons capers
12 very thin lemon slices
½ cup dry white wine

Place each fillet on a piece of lettuce and put salt, pepper, dillweed, and capers on each. Place three lemon slices on top and cover with a second piece of lettuce, tucking it under. Arrange in a single layer in a baking dish, pour wine over top, and bake 25 minutes at 350 degrees. Serves 4.

Fred Warner's German Restaurant

Route 220 South
CRESAPTOWN

During President John F. Kennedy's administration, a taxi arrived at Fred Warner's German Restaurant one day to pick up two "Bee Sting" Cakes. They were then transported by airplane and helicopter to the White House. Few people get that kind of delivery service, but the Bienstich, or "Bee Sting," Cakes are very popular at Fred Warner's. "The people like them gooey," Warner says, so he puts in lots of honey, rum, and black walnuts. Also justly famous are his Apple Strudels and loaves of fresh-baked Rye Bread.

Meals
11:30 A.M. until 9:00 P.M.
Tuesday through Saturday

Noon until 7:00 P.M.
Sunday

For reservations
(accepted, but not necessary)
call (301) 729-2361

The rye flour used for the bread comes from the 1877 gristmill that Fred Warner, Sr., used to operate in West Virginia. And on the Rye Bread go slices of Ham prepared the way Fred's father did it: baked with rings of pineapple, maraschino cherries, and sweet, spicy cloves. So "Ham on Rye" says something special at Fred Warner's—something about the value of family and carrying on traditions.

"Mountain people are my kind of people," Fred said as he described the German valley in West Virginia where his mother's home, a log house with a tin roof, was built during the Civil War. He named a creamy yellow salad dressing "Hansel Mountain Mamma Dressing" for his "mountain mamma" and his brother Hansel, who worked in the gristmill. When the mill was sold in 1928, the Warners built the building in Cresaptown that was first a grocery store and is now Fred Warner's German Restaurant.

The restaurant is intimate and informal. "*Willkommen*" is spoken here in an arborlike dining room where bunches of grapes hang from the ceiling. Gordon and I were at Fred Warner's for lunch, and we sampled Salad Bar offerings spread over several checked tablecloths. We could easily have made a meal just from cold Potato Salad, Cheese Bread, and Apple Butter. I tried several different dressings over bits of spinach and lettuce. Naturally, my favorite was Hansel Mountain Mamma. It was oniony and sweet.

While we ate our salads, Fred Warner and his wife, Marian, brought a bottle of May wine to our table with the best Wiener Schnitzel I have ever eaten. The secret seems to be in grinding the veal cutlets very fine and coating them with crumbs processed from homemade bread. With the veal, we ate crunchy Potato Pancakes, Sauerkraut, and cold Apfelmus (applesauce). I like sauerkraut even straight from a can, but when it's cooked with pork ribs and apples, it earns its reputation as a good German vegetable.

It was a "glorious evening," Fred said, when forty-seven Germans on business in this country came to the restaurant, starved for a good German dinner. They listened to country-and-western music while they ate, and later they wrote to say it was a highlight of their itinerary. A highlight of *your* trip to Maryland might be one of the four yearly festivals at Fred Warner's, with bite-size desserts, general feasting, dancing, and German bands from Washington. *Wunderbar!*

FRED WARNER'S GERMAN RESTAURANT'S APPLE STRUDEL

Dough

½ tablespoon butter, melted	½ cup warm water
1 egg, beaten	2 cups all-purpose flour

Mix together butter, egg, and water. Work in enough flour to make a soft dough. Make into a small, round loaf. Place loaf on a plate and cover it with waxed paper for 30 minutes.

Filling

5 cups sliced apples	½ cup raisins
½ cup brown sugar	2 tablespoons butter
½ teaspoon cinnamon	

Put a large cloth on a flat surface and sprinkle flour on the cloth. Stretch dough on the cloth until it is very thin. Spread apples on dough. Sprinkle with brown sugar, cinnamon, and raisins and dot with butter. Using edge of cloth, roll up dough like a jelly roll.

Place in a lightly greased 9- by 13-inch pan and bake in a 350-degree oven for 30 minutes. Ladle juices over strudel. Bake another 30 minutes and ladle again. Bake an additional 30 minutes (a total of 1½ hours) and remove from oven. Ladle juices over golden brown strudel and serve warm with cream, ice cream, or whipped cream. Serves 8.

FRED WARNER'S GERMAN RESTAURANT'S HANSEL MOUNTAIN MAMMA DRESSING

1 cup peanut oil
½ small onion, cut in chunks
1 cup sugar
¾ teaspoon prepared mustard

¼ teaspoon salt
½ cup white salad vinegar
½ teaspoon lemon juice

Put first 5 ingredients in a blender jar and mix on high speed for 2 minutes. Add vinegar and lemon juice and blend for a few seconds. Serve on sliced tomatoes, tossed salad, spinach, or other greens. Yields 1 pint.

FRED WARNER'S GERMAN RESTAURANT'S SAUERKRAUT

1 pound pork ribs
2 28-ounce cans sauerkraut,
   drained and rinsed
¼ cup sugar

¼ small onion, diced
½ teaspoon caraway seeds
1 unpeeled Red Delicious
   apple, chopped fine

Cover pork ribs with water and cook until tender. Remove ribs from broth, pick off lean meat, and return meat to broth. Add sauerkraut. Add remaining ingredients, cover, and simmer for about 1½ hours. Serves 8.

Au Petit Paris
Restaurant Français

86 East Main Street
FROSTBURG

$\mathscr{A}$ little bit of Paris is not what one would expect to find on Route 40 in western Maryland, but it's been here since 1960. It's a "special occasion" place for local diners—a woman outside the public library told me she thinks of it for graduation treats and anniversary parties.

Dinner
6:00 P.M. until 9:30 P.M.
Tuesday through Saturday

For reservations
(required)
call (301) 689-8946

But it is also a place for business people entertaining clients and for travelers looking for authentic French food.

The authenticity comes from the St. Marie family, which owns and operates Au Petit Paris Restaurant Français. The father (chef), mother (hostess), son (waiter), and daughter (bartender) do their jobs with polished efficiency.

For most of its years, the building—which burned and was rebuilt in the 1880s—was a furniture store. Deliveries were made by horse and wagon down the alley that is now the entrance to the restaurant. Guests enter a courtyard through a canopied door that separates Main Street from the experience of French dining.

Gordon and I found the whole meal, from frothy Crème Vichyssoise through Mousse au Chocolat Avec Grand Marnier, to be a special occasion. The bowls of Crème Vichyssoise were nestled in deep crystal plates of ice, with parsley garnishing both the ice and the delicately seasoned soup. The Mousse, with its distinctive taste of Grand Marnier, was topped with whipped cream and chocolate dots. I should tell you that we couldn't resist also dividing a slice of fresh, delicious Raspberry Cream Cake.

It was amazing that we ever reached dessert, having stuffed ourselves with Coq au Vin, whose name now seems as English as it does French. Of course, appetites grow on the strength of such good cooking, and ours were enhanced by a Louis Martini Pinot Noir selected from the extensive wine list.

Do you wonder, as I did, how the St. Maries happened to come to Frostburg? Au Petit Paris began as a club in Amarillo, Texas, for off-duty French air force personnel assigned to the jet aircraft school there. After Louis St. Marie left the air force and the school, he and his wife developed Au Petit Paris into a commercial restaurant and continued to operate it in Texas until 1959. Then they were approached by a citizen of Frostburg whose wife owned a dress shop in the building on Main Street. The St. Maries were invited to move Au Petit Paris to Frostburg, and they thought it was a good idea. Now, as their motto states, they are "Serving the World from Western Maryland."

AU PETIT PARIS RESTAURANT FRANÇAIS'S COQ AU VIN

3 to 4 slices bacon
6 to 8 pearl onions, peeled
6 small mushrooms
½ teaspoon sugar
1 teaspoon butter
1 whole chicken, cut into 6
    pieces
salt and pepper
flour for dredging
1 tablespoon olive oil

2 tablespoons cognac
1½ cups Burgundy
¾ cup chicken stock
1 large onion, chopped
1 clove garlic, crushed
1 sprig of thyme
½ teaspoon parsley, chopped
4 slices of garlic toast
2 sprigs of parsley

In a small saucepan, cook the bacon over low heat. Remove bacon and drain the fat into a larger pan, in which chicken will be sautéed. Add pearl onions, mushrooms, a little water, sugar, and butter to the smaller pan. Cover and cook over low heat until water has evaporated, shaking pan occasionally to assure everything is well coated. Set aside.

Season chicken pieces with salt and pepper and dredge in flour, shaking off excess. In the larger sauté pan, add olive oil to bacon fat. Place pan over medium heat, add chicken pieces skin side down, and sauté until chicken is golden brown. Turn pieces over and brown the other side.

Remove chicken to a platter, drain the pan of fat, and return chicken to pan. Add cognac and ignite, turning chicken pieces over quickly and with caution. Add Burgundy, chicken stock, chopped onion, garlic, thyme, and bacon strips. Cover and simmer over low heat for approximately 30 minutes. Remove chicken and set aside. Continue to reduce stock; if you desire a thicker stock, add a little cornstarch mixed with water. Place equal portions of chicken, mushrooms, and pearl onions on 2 warm plates. Strain sauce and pour over both portions. Sprinkle with chopped parsley and arrange 2 slices of garlic toast and a sprig of parsley on each plate. Serves 2.

AU PETIT PARIS RESTAURANT FRANÇAIS'S SCALLOPS BONNE FEMME

1 onion, minced
3 tablespoons butter
1 pound sea scallops
½ pound mushrooms, sliced
½ cup dry white wine
½ cup water
1 tablespoon lemon juice
3 tablespoons flour

salt and white pepper to taste
1 cup half-and-half
2 tablespoons Parmesan
   cheese, grated
2 tablespoons parsley, chopped
4 slices of toast, cut into
   points

Sauté onions in butter over medium heat until just tender. Add scallops, mushrooms, wine, water, and lemon juice. Reduce heat, cover, and simmer, taking care not to overcook the scallops. In a small bowl, blend flour, salt, white pepper, and half-and-half. Gradually stir in the scallops mixture. Continue to cook until mixture thickens.

To serve, place scallops into individual serving dishes. Sprinkle with Parmesan cheese and glaze under a broiler. Sprinkle each dish with parsley and place toast points on edge. Serves 4.

The Casselman

Main Street
GRANTSVILLE

arents, listen to your children. When thirteen-year-old Philip Miller saw a For Sale sign on the lawn of the old Casselman Hotel in 1964, he told his parents about the opportunity. The Ivan Millers, Mennonite farmers, were amused by their son's enthusiasm, but they investigated and decided to buy the property that an ancestor had owned almost a century earlier. With hard work and the common

Meals

7:00 A.M. until 8:00 P.M.
Monday through Thursday

7:00 A.M. until 9:00 P.M.
(10:00 P.M. in the summer)
Friday and Saturday

For reservations
(not necessary except
for large parties)
call (301) 895-5266

sense that comes from raising ten children, the Millers eventually developed the old hotel into an incorporated family business. They built a modern kitchen and reopened The Casselman's restaurant, which had been closed for twenty years; then they added a bakery and built a forty-room motor inn behind the hotel.

The Federal-style hotel, built of handmade bricks fired on the site, has gone by many names: Sterner's Tavern, Drover's Inn, Farmer's Hotel, Dorsey's Hotel, and The Casselman Hotel. It was built in 1824 to accommodate travelers on the Old National Road, now part of Route 40. Nowhere in my travels of that long highway have I been more impressed by its place in history than in Grantsville.

The road was first an Indian trail for packhorses and was called Nemacolin's Path. Later, it aided the military as a supply line and was named Braddock's Road, after the general who had it widened from six to twelve feet. It was called the Cumberland Road after Congress appropriated funds in 1806 to rebuild it from Cumberland, Maryland, to Wheeling, West Virginia—making it the first national highway.

When that same road brought Gordon and me to Grantsville, The Casselman's Dorsey Room was ready for us. We went right to sleep in a carved antique bed. I dreamed—or did I?—that someone slipped down the hall in the wee hours to start breakfast, and soon bakery smells wafted upstairs.

Those smells called us to breakfast in a dining room appropriately wallpapered with road scenes. The souvenir place mat that announced

"Rooms and Meals in a Quiet Country Atmosphere" gave equal space to facts about The Casselman and the Old National Road.

Gordon began the day with Oatmeal served with a dish of brown sugar. I was tempted by the peanut butter and jelly offered as an extra with an English Muffin, but I passed that up for one of the Cinnamon Buns that I smelled baking.

When I visited the bakery, which is located in the basement with a gift shop, I saw the popular Applesauce Nut Bread being made for takeout orders, as well as for use in the dining room. It's the fruity, nutty, spicy kind of bread that is as welcome as cake at our house.

The Casselman's cuisine is simple and substantial country food featuring a variety of favorite Amish recipes. Before leaving, we sampled two of the dishes prepared for lunch, Baked Beans and the ever-popular Shoofly Pie. The beans, baked with a tasty amount of catsup and brown sugar, seemed like a good dish to take to a church supper. The Casselman's Shoofly Pie calls for a filling of light and dark syrup, rather than cane molasses—a variation on the most famous Amish recipe of all.

THE CASSELMAN'S SHOOFLY PIE

Filling

½ teaspoon baking soda
¾ cup boiling water
½ cup dark corn syrup

½ cup light corn syrup
9-inch pie shell, unbaked

Dissolve soda in boiling water, then add syrups. Cool, then pour into pie shell.

Topping

1 cup flour
½ cup brown sugar

½ teaspoon baking soda
¼ cup shortening

Combine flour, sugar and baking soda. Using your fingers, rub shortening into flour mixture until crumbly. Spoon over filling. Bake pie in a 375-degree oven for approximately 35 minutes. Yields 1 pie.

THE CASSELMAN'S BAKED BEANS

2 cups navy beans or great
   northern beans, dried
1/2 cup brown sugar
1/4 cup catsup
1/2 small onion, chopped fine

1/8 teaspoon dry mustard
pinch of ginger
1/2 cup chopped ham or bacon
   bits
12-ounce can tomato juice

Soak beans in cold water for several hours or overnight, then cook until beans are almost soft. Add remaining ingredients; tomato juice should cover mixture. Bake in a 3-quart casserole or baking pan in a 325-degree oven for 45 minutes. Serves 8.

THE CASSELMAN'S APPLESAUCE NUT BREAD

2 eggs, slightly beaten
1 1/4 cups applesauce
3 tablespoons cooking oil
3/4 cup sugar
3/4 cup chopped nuts
2 cups all-purpose flour

1 tablespoon baking powder
1 teaspoon salt
1/2 teaspoon baking soda
3/4 teaspoon cinnamon
1/2 teaspoon cloves, ground

Combine ingredients in order given. Mix, but do not overbeat. Pour into a greased bread pan and bake at 375 degrees for 1 hour or until tester comes out clean. Yields one 1-pound loaf.

Penn Alps Restaurant

Route 40
GRANTSVILLE

Sometime in the 1830s, the keepers of the Inn at Little Crossings (later the Dixie Tavern and now Penn Alps Restaurant) got word from a stagecoach company to have plenty of beef and boiled potatoes ready at a certain time. Thirty prominent Indians on their way to see President Andrew Jackson would stop there for dinner. The inn also prepared turkeys for a party of white people due at the same time, but their coach ran late and couldn't stop, so the Indians feasted on both meats. What they ate at the inn on their way home is not recorded, but what they wore is interesting. The men had on broadcloth suits, and the one squaw wore a beaded dress — quite a contrast to the blankets they'd worn on their way to Washington.

November to Memorial Day
Meals
7:00 A.M. until 7:00 P.M.
Monday through Thursday

7:00 A.M. until 8:00 P.M.
Friday and Saturday

7:00 A.M. until 3:00 P.M.
Sunday

Memorial Day to November
Meals
7:00 A.M. until 8:00 P.M.
Monday through Saturday

7:00 A.M. until 3:00 P.M.
Sunday

For reservations
(not required)
call (301) 895-5985

Located in the old log stagecoach stop, constructed in 1818 and since remodeled, Penn Alps Restaurant and Craft Shop serves meals and shows such crafts as weaving, ceramics, and woodcarving—both the method and the finished product. The craft program helps the people of upper Appalachia market their handiwork and makes customers more aware of art processes. The day Gordon and I were there, a craftsman was carving birds so real we had to feel their feathers. He worked in one of several log cabins across from the main building while visitors strolled in to watch him.

Our walking tour also took in the Casselman River Bridge, the largest stone arch in America when it was built in 1813. George Washington forded the Casselman River in 1755 and named the area "The Little Crossings."

The founder of Penn Alps, Dr. Alta Schrock, pushed aside plants and books to get to my questions. She was preparing a nutrition lecture, she said, but "the Lord will help me put it together." I had the feeling that that had been her approach when she bought the place in 1959 and started a restaurant. She called a woman in from the kitchen to ask her about a recipe and introduced her warmly by saying, "I found her in a corn patch twenty-four years ago."

Gordon and I browsed the Craft Shop while visitors from a tour bus ate lunch. I was attracted to a pink chintz chicken with a red felt comb and brown rickrack braid. It was priced as reasonably as chickens I buy at the grocery store. I tucked it under my arm to add to my craft collection.

Most of the recipes used at Penn Alps are Pennsylvania Dutch. I asked how to prepare a favorite Pennsylvania Dutch vegetable, Dried Corn, thinking of some friends who have corn drying in their solar-heated greenhouse. Penn Alps uses a ton of dried corn a year, either cooking it in the restaurant or selling it by the pound in the Craft Shop.

For our late lunch at Penn Alps, Gordon and I ate a hearty German Vegetable Soup, crisp Coleslaw, and Applesauce spiced with cinnamon. A popular new dessert is Nut Brown Pudding, made from whatever bread is left over—even Applesauce Bread. I asked for the recipe, thinking it would be popular at our house, too.

PENN ALPS RESTAURANT'S DRIED CORN

1 cup dried corn	1 tablespoon sugar
6 cups water	4 tablespoons margarine
1/2 teaspoon salt	1/3 cup half-and-half

Simmer corn in water for 1 hour to reconstitute it. After corn has cooked, add salt, sugar, and margarine. Add half-and-half, stir until thoroughly heated, and serve. Serves 4.

PENN ALPS RESTAURANT'S CHICKEN STUFFING

1-pound loaf of bread
2 tablespoons butter
3 stalks celery, diced
1 onion, diced
½ teaspoon black pepper

¾ teaspoon poultry seasoning
2 cups chicken broth
3 eggs
½ cup ham, diced
½ cup American cheese, diced

Leave crust on bread; cut bread into cubes and set aside. Melt butter in a skillet. Add celery and onion and sauté until soft. Add pepper and poultry seasoning while cooking. Add the celery-and-onion mixture and the chicken broth to the bread. Beat eggs in a separate bowl and add to bread; mixture should be wet. Add ham and cheese to bread mixture. Combine well. Yields enough stuffing mixture to stuff two 5-pound chickens or 1 turkey.

PENN ALPS RESTAURANT'S NUT BROWN PUDDING

¼ pound margarine
2 cups sugar
½ teaspoon salt
1 teaspoon nutmeg
2 teaspoons cinnamon
1 teaspoon cloves, ground
2 eggs

½ cup flour
1½ teaspoons soda
¼ cup warm water
3¼ cups milk
4 cups bread, cubed
1 cup raisins
¾ cup chopped nuts

In a large mixing bowl, cream margarine, sugar, salt, and spices. Add eggs and beat until smooth, then add flour and the soda dissolved in warm water. In a separate bowl, pour milk over bread, raisins, and nuts. Combine the 2 mixtures and pour into a greased 9- by 13-inch pan. Bake at 300 degrees for 1 hour. Serves 12.

The Deer Park Inn

Deer Park Hotel Road
DEER PARK

"The house just spoke to us," Deborah Hamilton said. She and her husband, John Gonzales, were thinking of opening a restaurant closer to Deep Creek Lake when they found the Pennington Cottage, built around 1890. They couldn't resist the charm of the former summer house designed by Baltimore architect Josiah Pennington, especially when some of the original

Dinner
5:30 P.M. until 9:30 P.M.
Tuesday through Saturday
(Memorial Day to Labor Day)
Thursday through Saturday
(Labor Day to Memorial Day)

For reservations
(requested)
call (301) 334-2308

Victorian and Mission Oak furniture was also available to them. So their plan grew to include elegant country dining and guest accommodations.

Elegant dining was no obstacle. Both Deborah and John had been in the food business in Washington, D.C., Deborah planning banquets at the Hay-Adams and John serving as executive chef at the Watergate, the Ritz Carleton, and the Jockey Club. Restoring guest accommodations was harder, but the couple worked diligently.

The seventeen-room "cottage" was built when Deer Park Hotel was a famous resort. Prominent families spent their summers in cottages built around the hotel.

Gordon and I spent a night in one of The Deer Park Inn's guest rooms. I admired Josiah Pennington's design details: the bay of three windows, the beading on the wood, the small squares of rose and green tile around the fireplace.

We had dinner in a majestic room papered in red and green stripes with peacocks, fruit, and flowers. The setting was wonderful — fireplace, paneled wainscoting, a built-in china cabinet, and a built-on-site sideboard — but The Deer Park Inn's reason for being is its restaurant. We came away with fond memories of Tuscan Bean Soup, Scallop Salad with Snow Peas and Walnut Vinaigrette, and Frozen Grand Marnier Mousse with Apricot Sauce.

Breakfast was served in the Library. We enjoyed bacon with crisp-edged pancakes and conversation with Deborah. She said that the borne located in the entry was painted yellow when she found it in an antique shop, and that the carousel horse on the stair landing came from her aunt. I know I've described the house more than the food, but I'm saving room for recipes that speak for themselves. It was the house that spoke to Deborah and John, and I'm so glad they answered yes.

THE DEER PARK INN'S FROZEN GRAND MARNIER MOUSSE WITH APRICOT SAUCE

6 egg yolks
½ cup sugar
¼ cup water
3 tablespoons Grand Marnier liqueur

8 ounces sour cream
28-ounce can apricots in heavy syrup
3 tablespoons apricot brandy
fresh raspberries or strawberries

Whisk yolks, sugar, and water in a double boiler over boiling water for 4 to 5 minutes until thermometer reaches 160 degrees. Remove from double boiler and beat with an electric mixer about 5 minutes until cooled and very thick. Beat in Grand Marnier and add sour cream until blended. Pour mixture into six 6-ounce ramekins and freeze until firm.

Drain and purée apricots; add apricot brandy and enough syrup (about ½ cup) to make a smooth, thick sauce. Chill mixture.

To serve, dip ramekins briefly into hot water, run a knife around edge to loosen, and invert ramekins on serving plates. Spoon sauce around mousse; garnish with raspberries or strawberries. Serves 6.

THE DEER PARK INN'S TUSCAN BEAN SOUP

1 pound dry cannellini beans or great northern beans
3 cloves garlic, chopped
3 tablespoons olive oil
6 cups chicken stock

1 ham hock
1 pound canned tomatoes, crushed
salt and pepper to taste
Romano cheese, grated

Soak beans overnight in cold water. Sauté garlic in olive oil until golden. Drain beans and add to chicken stock; add garlic and ham hock. Add tomatoes and simmer for at least 2 hours. Add salt and pepper. Remove half of beans from soup and purée with a little broth; add back into soup to thicken. Add salt and pepper again. To serve, place soup in bowls and float a little olive oil on top. Sprinkle with Romano cheese. Serves 15.

THE DEER PARK INN'S SCALLOP SALAD WITH SNOW PEAS AND WALNUT VINAIGRETTE

1 pound sea scallops
salt and pepper to taste
1/2 pound snow peas
1 yellow bell pepper, julienned
1 green bell pepper, julienned
1 red bell pepper, julienned

1 pound mixed salad greens, washed and chilled
Walnut Vinaigrette (recipe below)
1/3 cup toasted walnuts, chopped

Clean scallops and pat dry. Season with salt and pepper. Sauté scallops in olive oil until just cooked. Steam snow peas until bright green and tender. Sauté peppers in 2 tablespoons of olive oil. Combine all cooked ingredients in a bowl and set aside.

To serve, divide salad greens among 8 plates. Top with scallop mixture. Pour Walnut Vinaigrette on each salad and top with walnuts. Serves 8.

Walnut Vinaigrette

2 shallots, chopped
1/4 cup red wine vinegar
1 teaspoon sugar

1/4 cup walnut oil
1/4 cup olive oil
salt and pepper to taste

Sauté shallots in 1 tablespoon of olive oil until softened. Add vinegar, sugar, walnut oil, olive oil, salt, and pepper. Simmer 1 minute. Let cool.

Cornish Manor

Memorial Drive (the old Deer Park Road)
OAKLAND

"If ever you had a thought to buy a country home, it would be wise to *see this*," said the elaborate real-estate brochure. In addition to an eighteen-room house on twenty acres referred to as "the most beautiful tract in Garrett County," this estate had crystal-pure water piped from town, electric lights, and a Bell telephone. Built in 1868 by a judge from Washington, the summer house was sold by its second owner when poor health required him to move to the city. At that time, the estate was called

Lunch
11:00 A.M. until 3:00 P.M.
Monday through Friday

Dinner
5:00 P.M. until 10:00 P.M.
Monday through Saturday

Sunday Brunch
11:00 A.M. until 3:00 P.M.
June through September

For reservations
(accepted)
call (301) 334-3551

Ethelhurst, named for the owner's daughter Ethel. Later owners gave it their name — Cornish — which the present owners kept.

We ate in the sun parlor on the front of the house, an enclosed portion of the 125-foot-long veranda. On an earlier visit, we had been told about Cornish Manor's ghost, and I was curious to see whether he still lived among the Victorian renovations made by new owners Christiane and Fred Bergheim. They said others, too, had inquired about the ghost, and all they could say was that they hadn't seen him.

Maybe they've been too busy to notice. Fred has a bakery at nearby Deep Creek Lake, and Christiane, believing that variety is the spice of life, is determined to keep surprises coming at Cornish Manor. They say their eight-ounce Hamburgers on sourdough bread are better than those at Club 21 in New York, and sometimes they have a Hamburger Half-Price Surprise. Specials are offered every day. The Rotary Club, which meets here one night a week, is never served the same thing twice. The day we were here, the Rotarians were to have Chili in a bread "boule" — Christiane is French — which sounded good to us. We knew the bread was delicious, having tasted both the sourdough and vegetable varieties. Cornish Manor scoops out six-inch round loaves to make bowls to fill with soup or warm Chicken Salad.

Gordon had the Chicken Salad with his bread, while I had the popular Chicken Barley Soup. You'd expect a restaurant called Cornish Manor to serve Cornish Hen; I got the recipe for the manor's version, served with a sauce made of honey mustard and cream. I was also glad to get the recipe for Red Snapper with Pecan Frangelico Sauce.

After lunch, we looked at the changes made in the décor of the dining rooms and the larger rooms upstairs, which can be reserved for private parties. Forsythia adorned most of the tables, as it had ours in the sun parlor. Piano music is provided on Friday and Saturday nights in the lobby at the foot of the stairs, where the ghost was once sighted. It occurred to me that Cornish Manor's ghost may not yet have gotten accustomed to Christiane's French accent or the new regime. Fred had another idea; the ghost may be in the attic studying Berlitz.

CORNISH MANOR'S RED SNAPPER WITH PECAN FRANGELICO SAUCE

8-ounce red snapper fillet
flour

salt and pepper to taste
2 ounces cooking oil

Coat snapper in flour; add salt and pepper. Sauté the fillet in hot oil for 2 minutes on each side until light brown. Remove from heat and place in a 350-degree oven to warm for 5 to 7 minutes.

Pecan Frangelico Sauce

2 tablespoons unsalted butter
1 tablespoon chopped pecans

2 tablespoons Frangelico
liqueur

Heat sauté pan over medium-high heat and cook butter until brown. Add pecans and Frangelico. Ignite and reduce until sauce is thick. Place warm snapper on a plate and top with sauce. Serves 1.

CORNISH MANOR'S CORNISH HEN

1½-pound Cornish hen
2 ounces cooking oil
salt and pepper
2 tablespoons honey mustard

4 tablespoons heavy cream
flour
parsley or green onions for
garnish

Place hen in a shallow baking pan and sprinkle with oil, salt, and pepper. Roast in a 350-degree oven for 1 hour and 15 minutes or until brown. In a sauté pan, combine honey mustard and cream, stirring over medium heat until bubbly. Add a pinch of flour if needed to thicken. Cut hen in half, putting 1 breast half on each of 2 plates. Top with sauce and garnish with parsley or green onions if desired. Serves 2.

CORNISH MANOR'S CHICKEN BARLEY SOUP

2 quarts chicken broth
¾ cup pearl barley
1 pound carrots, diced
4 stalks celery, diced

1 small onion, diced
1 cup cooked chicken, chopped
⅛ cup parsley, chopped
salt and pepper to taste

Bring chicken broth to a boil and add barley, carrots, celery, onion, and chicken. Cook on low heat for approximately 1 hour. Parsley may be cooked or used as a garnish. Add salt and pepper. Serves 6.

Note: Cornstarch may be used as a thickener; however, soup will thicken as it stands.

Index